love of Labs

From the Editors of
Voyageur Press

Foreword by
Field & Stream's Bill Tarrant

Voyageur Press

Compiled and edited by Todd R. Berger
Designed by Andrea Rud
Printed in Hong Kong

98 99 00 01 5 4 3 2

Library of Congress Cataloging-in-Publication Data
Love of Labs / from the editors of Voyageur Press.
        p.   cm.
   ISBN 0-89658-356-2
   1. Labrador retriever—Anecdotes. I. Voyageur Press.
  SF429.L3L68   1997
  636.752'7—dc21   97-7939
                  CIP

Published by Voyageur Press, Inc.
123 North Second Street, P.O. Box 338, Stillwater, MN 55082 U.S.A.
612-430-2210, fax 612-430-2211

Educators, fundraisers, premium and gift buyers, publicists, and marketing managers: Looking for creative products and new sales ideas? Voyageur Press books are available at special discounts when purchased in quantities, and special editions can be created to your specifications. For details contact the marketing department at 800-888-9653.

Permissions
We have made every effort to determine original sources and locate copyright holders of the excerpts in this book. Grateful acknowledgment is made to the writers, publishers, and agencies listed below for permission to reprint material copyrighted or controlled by them. Please bring to our attention any errors of fact, omission, or copyright.
"The Dustbin Dog" from *The Lord God Made Them All* by James Herriot. Copyright © 1981 by James Herriot. Reprinted by permission of St. Martin's Press Incorporated. Reprinted in the United Kingdom and the Commonwealth by permission of David Higham Associates for Michael Joseph Limited.
"All Ghosts Aren't White" by Mel Ellis. Copyright © 1956 by Henry Holt & Co. Reprinted by permission of the Larry Sternig/ Jack Byrne Agency.
"Tale of the Bewildered Bird Dog" by David Morine. Copyright © 1990 by David Morine. Reprinted by permission of the Fifi Oscard Agency, Inc.
"One" by Gene Hill. Copyright © 1981 by Gene Hill. Reprinted by permission of the author.
"Bess' Story" by John Madson. Copyright © 1995 by John Madson. Reprinted by permission of Dycie Madson.
"Old One-Ear" by Dion Henderson. Copyright © 1953 by Henry Holt & Co. Reprinted by permission of the Larry Sternig/ Jack Byrne Agency.
"Of Miracles and Memories" from *Pick of the Litter* by Bill Tarrant. Copyright © 1995 by Bill Tarrant. Reprinted by permission of Lyons & Burford, Publishers.

Page 1: *A black Labrador retriever in flooded timber.* Photo © Lon E. Lauber
Page 2–3: *A beautiful black Lab holds a retrieving dummy.* Photo © William H. Mullins
Page 3: *Two Lab puppies go to battle over a highly desirable dirty washrag.* Photo © Alan and Sandy Carey
Facing page: *Labs come in a wide range of shades. This yellow Lab pup looks almost white.* Photo © Kent and Donna Dannen
Page 6: *Posing in a field of wildflowers, a black Lab basks in radiant sunshine.* Photo © Bruce Montagne

Contents

Foreword

by Bill Tarrant

 Ancient Egypt was the only civilization to worship a dog. His name was Anubis, and in early tomb paintings he bears the likeness of a jackal, but later depictions show him remarkably like a basenji.

Anubis was the fourth-ranked god in the Egyptian holy order. His function was to give safe passage to the deceased, guiding them to a judge who would decree the soul's eternal estate. Then Anubis would remain to care for the departed.

Since ancient Egypt, the only civilizations to accord the dog a status approximate to Anubis are modern North America and Great Britain. And that is evident in their love of Labs. No, they don't worship the Lab, but I think there are some who liken their dogs to angels.

Wouldn't you, if you couldn't see, and the Lab led you? Or if you couldn't hear, and the Lab heard for you? What does an angel do if not these things?

Longtime gun dog patron Bob Wehle wrote in his book, *Snakefoot: The Making of a National Champion,* "I have so much respect for the purity of their character and the sincerity of their everlasting devotion." Bob was speaking of English pointers, which are his love, but for me, the quote describes the Labrador retriever.

When my wife and I first moved to the sun-splashed, Sonoran desert, she used to say, "It makes me feel like gold." That's the way a Lab makes me feel. Their essence radiates through their pores.

"Labs are probably the most indispensable dogs on earth." Bill Tarrant. Photo © William H. Mullins

I remember FC and AFC Keg of Black Powder and her human partner, Jim Culbertson, who was making $4,000 a year as a football coach for the Mulvane, Kansas, high school in 1964. Powder was a miracle performer. Never has there been another field trial contender like her.

Being so exceptional, Powder gave men who covet honor the notion that if they could buy her, they could win the silver bowl denoting the National Championship and a bit of immortality for themselves.

Such a man offered Jim $18,500 for the little black bitch. And what does that amount to, more than four years salary?

Jim said no. And Powder died in poverty with the man she loved. The richest poverty a dog and man ever shared.

But don't think Labrador retrievers have value and are prided only by field trial contenders and bird hunters. Labs are special in many ways. Labs are probably the most indispensable dogs on earth.

I was visiting a friend in the hospital and here came one of those therapy Labs. The lady with the dog approached my friend's bed, and the Lab laid his big black head on the covers, raised those whiskey-colored eyes.

My friend smiled. Every sick or injured person seems to smile when a Lab enters the room.

I've since learned when a Lab becomes a permanent resident at a care facility, prescription consumption goes down, depression fades, those who have shut themselves off from the world decide to mix and talk again, and things just start being cheery and promising.

I once knew an arson inspector who worked for an insurance agency. Suspecting arson in a lumber mill fire, he traveled to Oregon, and I tagged along. His Lab slid out of the car with no real show of motivation and began sniffing the burnt sawdust. In no time at all he was on to something. Then the Lab alerted on a fire starter, and the inspector saved his company a lot of money.

Other Labs have dug through avalanches, through debris of bombed buildings, through the destruction of earthquakes, to recover people who would otherwise have perished.

Labs patrol post offices, airports, and customs entries to detect contraband.

As noted, they listen for the deaf, see for the blind.

They pick up the ringing telephone, turn off the light switch, open the refrigerator door, and much more, for the paralyzed person in a wheelchair or bed.

So much of what they do is because of their miraculous scent. The border patrol at Otay Mesa, California, has told me a Lab-mix named Snag scented through a steel tanker of propane, and on through the horribly stinking additive of ethylmercaptan, which is used so we can detect leaks, since propane is odorless. Snag uncovered 8,705 pounds (3,917 kg) of cocaine with a street value of $564 million.

A Southern dermatologist predicts Labs will one day detect skin

Facing page, top: *The Labrador retriever is the leading breed in use as a guide dog for the blind.* Photo © Tara Darling

Facing page, bottom: *"Its other achievements aside, the Lab excels most of all as a pet. It's a down-to-earth dog with old-fashioned virtues—loyalty, courage, calmness, imperviousness to pain or adversity, application to the task at hand, and a love of family, rugged pleasures and simple comforts." Wendy Insinger.* Photo © Tara Darling

cancer on patients.

And what about the regular old house Lab? Those who have turned away intruders, awakened families to dense smoke, and thrown themselves before more than one child approaching a rattlesnake, or pulled other children from the family swimming pool.

The truth is, the Labrador retriever can feed you, heal you, defend you, help you, delight you, comfort you . . .

You hold in your hand a story book written by Lab-smitten people, and displaying remarkable pictures by photographers who have also succumbed to the dog's aura. Writers and photographers who have been captivated by that mellow warmth that all Labs transmit, to the softness of their petal-shaped ears, the wisdom and kindness radiated by their deep amber eyes, to that clump of muscle arching over the massive shoulders that is so great to take in hand and chug in playful jest.

In this book there is death and birth, sadness and joy, loss and gain, hope and despair, plus much that is odd, and more that is predictable. Because pen and lens never strayed from the truth, the core essence of the Lab is depicted here.

Plus I can tell you this. Those who contributed to this book's existence loved every moment of their labor. For after all, it was all done for the love of Labs.

Join us now as we go toe-to-tail to freedom's call, wandering through print and picture, with the greatest dog of all.

Bill Tarrant is the Gun Dog Editor for *Field & Stream* magazine.

A hearty pair of black Labs just after a swim in the Pacific Ocean. Photo © Alan and Sandy Carey

[A Lab is] a kind of perpetual five-year-old, forever young, forever loving.
—James Michener

Introduction

 There are few things that can get as close to a human heart as a dog. Whether it is a big-ole head lying in your lap as you read the Sunday paper on the couch; a loafer reduced to a toothmarked, shredded, loose conglomeration of cowskin; ridiculous amounts of chow chomp-chomped in an oversize, awkward jaw; or a dripping shadow delivering a duck to hand, dogs are a part of us. Frankly, a dog is our best friend. And the dog that is the best friend of more people than any other is, without question, the Labrador retriever.

By the mid-1990s, more than 130,000 Labs were registered with the American Kennel Club, outdistancing the breed's closest rival, the Rottweiler, by nearly 40,000 dogs. And this is only the registered Labs. Countless other Labradors—some of dubious pedigree— inhabit the backyard kennels and living-room carpets of the world. Registered Labrador retrievers also rank at the top with the Canadian Kennel Club, while in Great Britain, where the breed as we know it today was developed, Queen Elizabeth II keeps a kennel of Labs. The Lab is the top show and field dog in Britain. As Bill Tarrant put it, "big men with big yellow Labs are nearly as common in England as tweed coats."

Not to be outdone by a reigning monarch, people as diverse as Bob Dylan, Henry Kissinger, Barbara Mandrell, and Nicolae Ceausescu, the former communist dictator of Romania, all had Labs. If we could get a cross section of Lab owners together for a cocktail party, it would be a memorable evening indeed.

A pheasant hunter praises his Lab after a job well done. Photo © William H. Mullins

Whether they utilize them as full-fledged gun dogs to retrieve downed mallards or Canada geese, as convenient footrests while they check the Dow, or as mannequins manipulated into dresses by packs of giggling, seven-year-olds, people love their Labs. As Gene Hill wrote: "A Lab is the perfect fishing companion, an ideal partner for visiting country saloons, a never-bored buddy for a long trip, a creature whose tastes in music embrace it all from Willie Nelson to W. A. Mozart." It is this laid-back, devoted nature that endears the Lab to us.

A Brief History of the Lab

The ascendancy of the Labrador retriever has been rapid, particularly in the United States. The Lab didn't arrive in serious numbers in the U.S. until the 1920s and 1930s, although the breed enjoyed great popularity in England beginning in the early nineteenth century.

The Labrador retriever took a circuitous route to U.S. shores, as its traceable origins lie up the eastern coast in the Canadian province of Newfoundland. The Labrador retriever was known there in the early nineteenth century as the St. John's Newfoundland (a smaller cousin of today's Newfoundland breed), and earned its keep carrying lines between fishing vessels and from the boats to shore. The hearty dogs carried the lines in heavy, North Atlantic seas, eagerly leaping into icy

Best to turn over an old tennis shoe to your new Lab pup, otherwise the youngster may focus on your leather loafers. Photo © William H. Mullins

waters that would give a mere human hypothermia. They worked for their masters, serving a vital role in a rugged, unforgiving environment.

At some time around 1820, the Second Earl of Malmesbury, a noted British sportsman of his day, is believed to have purchased several of these retrievers from Newfoundland fishing boats docked at Poole Harbour, Dorset, England. At the time, English hunters were retrieving game primarily with pointers, setters, and water spaniels. But the superior talent for waterfowling of this imported Newfoundland breed quickly became apparent, and the dog gained rapid favor among British hunters. Colonel Peter Hawker, another leading sportsman of the era, is credited as the first to refer to the dogs as "Labradors," and the name stuck, even though the dogs did not actually come from Labrador.

Around the turn of the century, Labs were brought back to North America, at first in small numbers. By 1930, the breed was winning many admirers in the United States, and a steady stream of dogs flowed into the country. The endearing qualities of this efficient working dog helped boost its popularity. In 1942, William F. Brown, editor of *The American Field*, wrote: "There is an external calmness about the dog that radiates confidence in his ability to do what is desired of him. A serenity of disposition that makes the Labrador an excellent companion. . . . Even those [Labs] which exude great keenness and fire, outwardly are imperturbable and seemingly seek to learn only what the master requires, then endeavor to do the job thoroughly, expeditiously." This first-class retriever with an unflappable, loyal personality quickly won the hearts of the Americans, just as it had of the British a century earlier and of the Newfoundland fishermen before that.

Yellow Labs, such as this one retrieving a stick, have officially been around since the turn of the century. Ben of Hyde, the first recognized yellow Labrador retriever, was whelped in England in 1899.
Photo © Alan and Sandy Carey

About *Love of Labs*

Not surprisingly, much of the American, Canadian, and British literature about the breed emphasizes the hunting skill of the Labrador. To many of the authors, writing about Labrador retrievers without mentioning hunting would be akin to writing about the Olympic weight-lifting teams of the former Soviet Union without mentioning weight lifting.

Indeed, most of the stories and articles in this collection are tied in some way to the hunt, with the exception of James Herriot's piece, "The Dustbin Dog." But the focus is, without exception, on the Lab and the gentle nature and wonderful spirit of this most remarkable breed. Other themes of this book include the deep connection between owner and Lab, as in Bill Tarrant's "Of Miracles and Memories," in which that connection becomes a metaphor for life itself; and an abhorrence of cruelty to dogs, most evident in Mel Ellis's "All Ghosts Aren't White." This anthology also includes a funny-looking Lab that saves the life of a skeptical owner with a broken leg in "Old One-Ear," and "Bess' Story," the true tale of a Lab that keeps on working for her owner under the most trying circumstances. And if you think the field trial circuit is made up of hardened owners driving dogs to perfection, read about "One" and his owner in Gene Hill's piece, the story of a talented Lab and the transformation of his master in the face of tragedy.

This is also a book of images, and the photographers capture the spirit of the Labrador retriever with unrivaled clarity and talent. Featured here is the work of Bill Buckley, Alan and Sandy Carey, Kent and Donna Dannen, Tara Darling, Gary Kramer, Lon E. Lauber, Jack Macfarlane, Bill Marchel, Bruce Montagne, William H. Mullins, and Jim Schlender. Even if you never read a word of the text, you will love this book.

So build a fire, curl up in a corner of the couch, let your Lab up on the furniture so he can lay his head in your lap, and enjoy.

Below: *A winter sunset in the American West silhouettes the stout body of a black Lab.* Photo © William H. Mullins
Facing page: *A chocolate Labrador pauses along an autumn cornfield.* Photo © Lon E. Lauber

[My yellow Lab] Sweetzer, who is a timid dog, terrified even of certain varieties of fruit (particularly canteloupe, which she seems to think are small round aliens), was startled by the man and began howling at him, her hackles up, her front legs planted stiffly. All across the country, I would be apologizing for this goofy behavior of hers.
—Jim Fergus, *A Hunter's Road*, 1992

the Dustbin Dog

by James Herriot

Veterinarian and author James Herriot did not write his first book until he was into his fifth decade, but since the publication of *All Creatures Great and Small* in the 1970s, his wonderful essays on his many years in veterinary practice and his stories for children have made him one of the most cherished writers of the twentieth century. Scottish by birth, Herriot practiced veterinary medicine in Yorkshire, England, where he wrote many of his books, including *All Things Bright and Beautiful*, *All Things Wise and Wonderful*, *The Lord God Made Them All*, *Every Living Thing*, and *James Herriot's Yorkshire*. His books for children include *Moses the Kitten*, *Only One Woof*, and *The Market Square Dog*, among numerous others. Herriot always portrayed the animals he wrote about in a humane and loving voice.

This selection, which originally appeared in *The Lord God Made Them All* and was later published in *James Herriot's Dog Stories*, features the awkward and goofy yellow Lab Brandy, who will tickle your funnybone with his classic Labrador antics.

"[Brandy] was one of my patients, a huge, lolloping, slightly goofy animal . . ." James Herriot. Photo © William H. Mullins

IN THE SEMI-DARKNESS of the surgery passage I thought it was a hideous growth dangling from the side of the dog's face, but as he came closer, I saw that it was only a condensed milk can. Not that condensed milk cans are commonly found sprouting from dogs' cheeks, but I was relieved because I knew I was dealing with Brandy again.

I hoisted him onto the table. "Brandy, you've been at the dustbin again."

The big golden Labrador gave me an apologetic grin and did his best to lick my face. He couldn't manage it since his tongue was jammed inside the can, but he made up for it by a furious wagging of tail and rear end.

"Oh, Mr. Herriot, I am sorry to trouble you again." Mrs. Westby, his attractive young mistress, smiled ruefully. "He just won't keep out of that dustbin. Sometimes the children and I can get the cans off ourselves, but this one is stuck fast. His tongue is trapped under the lid."

"Yes . . . yes . . ." I eased my finger along the jagged edge of the metal. "It's a bit tricky, isn't it? We don't want to cut his mouth."

As I reached for a pair of forceps, I thought of the many other occasions when I had done something like this for Brandy. He was one of my patients, a huge, lolloping, slightly goofy animal, but this dustbin raiding was becoming an obsession.

He liked to fish out a can and lick out the tasty remnants, but his licking was carried out with such dedication that he burrowed deeper and deeper until he got stuck. Again and again he had been freed by his family or myself from fruit salad cans, corned beef cans, baked bean cans, soup cans. There didn't seem to be any kind of can he didn't like.

I gripped the edge of the lid with my forceps and gently bent it back along its length till I was able to lift it away from the tongue. An instant later, that tongue was slobbering all over my cheek as Brandy expressed his delight and thanks.

"The more I see of men, the better I like my dog." Frederick the Great.
Photo © Alan and Sandy Carey

"Get back, you daft dog!" I said, laughing, as I held the panting face away from me.

"Yes, come down, Brandy." Mrs. Westby hauled him from the table and spoke sharply. "It's all very fine, making a fuss now, but you're becoming a nuisance with this business. It will have to stop."

The scolding had no effect on the lashing tail, and I saw that his mistress was smiling. You just couldn't help liking Brandy because he was a great ball of affection and tolerance, without an ounce of malice in him.

I had seen the Westby children—there were three girls and a boy—carrying him around by the legs, upside down, or pushing him in a pram, sometimes dressed in baby clothes. Those youngsters played all sorts of games with him, but he suffered them all with good humour. In fact, I am sure he enjoyed them.

Brandy had other idiosyncracies, apart from his fondness for dustbins.

"You just couldn't help liking Brandy because he was a great ball of affection and tolerance, without an ounce of malice in him."

I was attending the Westby cat at their home one afternoon when I noticed the dog acting strangely. Mrs. Westby was sitting, knitting in an armchair, while the oldest girl squatted on the hearth rug with me and held the cat's head.

It was when I was searching my pockets for my thermometer that I noticed Brandy slinking into the room. He wore a furtive air as he moved across the carpet and sat down with studied carelessness in front of his mistress. After a few moments he began to work his rear end gradually up the front of the chair towards her knees. Absently, she took a hand away from her knitting and pushed him down, but he immediately restarted his backward ascent. It was an extraordinary mode of progression, his hips moving in a very slow rumba rhythm as he elevated them inch by inch, and all the time the golden face was blank and innocent, as though nothing at all were happening.

Fascinated, I stopped hunting for my thermometer and watched. Mrs. Westby was absorbed in an intricate part of her knitting and didn't seem to notice that Brandy's bottom was now firmly parked on her shapely knees which were clad in blue jeans. The dog paused, as though acknowledging that phase one had been successfully completed, then ever so gently he began to consolidate his position, pushing his way up the front of the chair with his fore limbs, till at one time he was almost standing on his head.

It was at that moment, just when one final backward heave would have seen the great dog ensconced on her lap, that Mrs. Westby finished the tricky bit of knitting and looked up.

"Oh, really, Brandy, you are silly!" She put a hand on his rump and sent him slithering disconsolately to the carpet, where he lay and looked at her with liquid eyes.

"What was all that about?" I asked.

Mrs. Westby laughed. "Oh, it's these old blue jeans. When Brandy first came here as a tiny puppy, I spent hours nursing him on my knee, and I used to wear the jeans a lot then. Ever since, even though he's a grown dog, the very sight of the things makes him try to get on my knee."

"But he doesn't just jump up?"

"Oh, no," she said. "He's tried it and got ticked off. He knows perfectly well I can't have a huge Labrador in my lap."

"So now it's the stealthy approach, eh?"

She giggled. "That's right. When I'm preoccupied—knitting or reading—sometimes he manages to get nearly all the way up, and if he's been playing in the mud he makes an awful mess, and I have to go and change. That's when he really does receive a scolding."

A patient like Brandy added colour to my daily round. When I was walking my own dog, I often saw him playing in the fields by the river. One particularly hot day many of the dogs were taking to the water, either to chase sticks or just to cool off, but whereas they glided in and swam off sedately, Brandy's approach was quite unique.

I watched as he ran up to the river bank, expecting him to pause before entering. But, instead, he launched himself outwards, legs splayed in a sort of swallow dive, and hung for a moment in the air rather like a flying fox before splashing thunderously into the depths. To me it was the action of a completely happy extrovert.

On the following day in those same fields I witnessed something even more extraordinary. There is a little children's playground in one corner—a few swings, a roundabout and a slide. Brandy was disporting himself on the slide.

For this activity he had assumed an uncharacteristic gravity of expression and stood calmly in the queue of children. When his turn came he mounted the steps, slid down the metal slope, all dignity and importance, then took a staid walk round to rejoin the queue.

The little boys and girls who were his companions seemed to take him for granted, but I found it difficult to tear myself away. I could have watched him all day.

I often smiled to myself when I thought of Brandy's antics, but I didn't smile when Mrs. Westby brought him into the surgery a few months later. His bounding ebullience had disappeared, and he dragged himself along the passage to the consulting room.

As I lifted him onto the table, I noticed that he had lost a lot of weight.

"Now, what is the trouble, Mrs. Westby?" I asked.

She looked at me worriedly. "He's been off-colour for a few days now, listless and coughing and not eating very well, but this morning he seems quite ill, and you can see he's starting to pant."

"Yes . . . yes . . ." As I inserted the thermometer I watched the rapid rise and fall of the rib cage and noted the gaping mouth and anxious eyes. "He does look very sorry for himself."

Temperature was 104. I took out my stethoscope and ausculated his lungs. I have heard of an old Scottish doctor describing a seriously ill patient's chest as sounding like a "kist o' whustles" and that just about described Brandy's. Râles, wheezes, squeaks and bubblings—they were all there against a background of laboured respiration.

I put the stethoscope back in my pocket. "He's got pneumonia."

"Oh, dear." Mrs. Westby reached out and touched the heaving chest. "That's bad, isn't it?"

"Yes, I'm afraid so."

"But . . ." She gave me an appealing glance. "I understand it isn't so fatal since the new drugs came out."

I hesitated. "Yes, that's quite right. In humans and most animals the sulpha drugs, and now penicillin, have changed the picture completely, but dogs are still very difficult to cure."

Thirty years later it is still the same. Even with all the armoury of antibiotics that followed penicillin—streptomycin, the tetracyclines, the synthetics and the new non-antibiotic drugs and steroids—I still hate to see pneumonia in a dog.

"But you don't think it's hopeless?" Mrs. Westby asked.

"No, no, not at all. I'm just warning you that so many dogs don't respond to treatment when they should. But Brandy is young and strong. He must stand a fair chance. I wonder what started this off, anyway."

"Oh, I think I know, Mr. Herriot. He had a swim in the river about a week ago. I try to keep him out of the water in this cold weather, but if he sees a stick floating, he just takes a dive into the middle. You've seen him—it's one of the funny little things he does."

"Yes, I know. And was he shivery afterwards?"

"He was. I walked him straight home, but it was such a freezing-cold day. I could feel him trembling as I dried him down."

I nodded. "That would be the cause, all right. Anyway, let's start his treatment. I'm going to give him this injection of penicillin, and I'll call at your house tomorrow to repeat it. He's not well enough to come to the surgery."

"Very well, Mr. Herriot. And is there anything else?"

"Yes, there is. I want you to make him what we call a pneumonia jacket. Cut two holes in an old blanket for his forelegs and stitch him into it along his back. You can use an old sweater if you like, but he must have his chest warmly covered. Only let him out in the garden for necessities."

I called and repeated the injection on the following day. There

Should a child decide to use the slide, this mellow Lab pup will get quite a surprise. Photo © Kent and Donna Dannen

wasn't much change. I injected him for four more days, and the realisation came to me sadly that Brandy was like so many of the others—he wasn't responding. The temperature did drop a little, but he ate hardly anything and grew gradually thinner. I put him on sulphapyridine tablets, but they didn't seem to make any difference.

As the days passed and he continued to cough and pant and to sink deeper into a blank-eyed lethargy, I was forced more and more to a conclusion which, a few weeks ago, would have seemed impossible—that this happy, bounding animal was going to die.

But Brandy didn't die. He survived. You couldn't put it any higher than that. His temperature came down and his appetite improved, and he climbed onto a plateau of twilight existence where he seemed content to stay.

"He isn't Brandy anymore," Mrs. Westby said one morning a few weeks later when I called in. Her eyes filled with tears as she spoke.

I shook my head. "No, I'm afraid he isn't. Are you giving him the halibut liver oil?"

"Yes, every day. But nothing seems to do him any good. Why is he like this, Mr. Herriot?"

"Well, he has recovered from a really virulent pneumonia, but it's left him with a chronic pleurisy, adhesions and probably other kinds of lung damage. It looks as though he's just stuck there."

She dabbed at her eyes. "It breaks my heart to see him like this. He's only five, but he's like an old, old dog. He was so full of life, too." She sniffed and blew her nose. "When I think of how I used to scold him for getting into the dustbins and muddying up my jeans. How I wish he would do some of his funny old tricks now."

I thrust my hands deep into my pockets. "Never does anything like that now, eh?"

"No, no, just hangs about the house. Doesn't even want to go for a

walk."

As I watched, Brandy rose from his place in the corner and pottered slowly over to the fire. He stood there for a moment, gaunt and dead-eyed, and he seemed to notice me for the first time because the end of his tail gave a brief twitch before he coughed, groaned and flopped down on the hearth rug.

Mrs. Westby was right. He was like a very old dog.

"Do you think he'll always be like this?" she asked.

I shrugged. "We can only hope."

But as I got into my car and drove away, I really didn't have much hope. I had seen calves with lung damage after bad pneumonias. They recovered but were called "bad doers" because they remained thin and listless for the rest of their lives. Doctors, too, had plenty of "chesty"

King George V was the first British monarch to breed Labradors. The tradition is carried on by his grand-daughter, Queen Elizabeth II.
Photo © Kent and Donna Dannen

people on their books; they were, more or less, in the same predicament.

Weeks and then months went by, and the only time I saw the Labrador was when Mrs. Westby was walking him on his lead. I always had the impression that he was reluctant to move, and his mistress had to stroll along very slowly so that he could keep up with her. The sight of him saddened me when I thought of the lolloping Brandy of old, but I told myself that at least I had saved his life. I could do no more for him now, and I made a determined effort to push him out of my mind.

In fact, I tried to forget Brandy and managed to do so fairly well until one afternoon in February. On the previous night I felt I had been through the fire. I had treated a colicky horse until 4 A.M. and was crawling into bed, comforted by the knowledge that the animal was settled down and free from pain, when I was called to a calving. I had managed to produce a large live calf from a small heifer, but the effort had drained the last of my strength, and when I got home, it was too late to return to bed.

Ploughing through the morning round, I was so tired that I felt disembodied, and at lunch Helen watched me anxiously as my head nodded over my food.

There were a few dogs in the waiting room at two o'clock, and I dealt with them mechanically, peering through half-closed eyelids.

By the time I reached my last patient, I was almost asleep on my feet. In fact, I had the feeling that I wasn't there at all.

There was a man in the doorway all right, and he had a little poodle with him, but the thing that made my eyes snap wide open was that the dog was walking upright on his hind limbs.

"Next, please," I mumbled as I pushed open the waiting-room door and stood back, expecting the usual sight of a dog being led out to the passage.

But this time there was a big difference. There was a man in the doorway all right, and he had a little poodle with him, but the thing that made my eyes snap wide open was that the dog was walking upright on his hind limbs.

I knew I was half-asleep, but surely I wasn't seeing things. I stared down at the dog, but the picture hadn't changed. The little creature strutted through the doorway, chest out, head up, as erect as a soldier.

"Follow me, please," I said hoarsely and set off over the tiles to the consulting room. Halfway along, I just had to turn round to check the evidence of my eyes, and it was just the same—the poodle, still on his hind legs, marching along unconcernedly at his master's side.

The man must have seen the bewilderment in my face because he burst suddenly into a roar of laughter.

"Don't worry, Mr. Herriot," he said. "This little dog was circus-trained before I got him as a pet. I like to show off his little tricks. This one really startles people."

"You can say that again," I said breathlessly. "It nearly gave me heart failure."

The poodle wasn't ill; he just wanted his nails clipped. I smiled as I hoisted him onto the table and began to ply the clippers.

"I suppose he won't want his hind claws doing," I said. "He'll have worn them down himself." I was glad to find I had recovered sufficiently to attempt a little joke.

However, by the time I had finished, the old lassitude had taken over again, and I felt ready to fall down as I showed man and dog to the front door.

I watched the little animal trotting away down the street—in the

A yellow Labrador puppy holds on tight to a stick, which is slightly longer than the pup itself. Photo © Alan and Sandy Carey

Like Brandy, this yellow Lab has a formidable tongue. Prepare to be licked! Photo © Jack Macfarlane

orthodox manner this time—and it came to me suddenly that it had been a long time since I had seen a dog doing something unusual and amusing. Like the things Brandy used to do.

A wave of gentle memories flowed through me as I leaned wearily against the doorpost and closed my eyes. When I opened them, I saw Brandy coming round the corner of the street with Mrs. Westby. His nose was entirely obscured by a large, red tomato-soup can, and he strained madly at the leash and whipped his tail when he saw me.

It was certainly a hallucination this time. I was looking into the past. I really ought to go to bed immediately. But I was still rooted to the doorpost when the Labrador bounded up the steps, made an attempt, aborted by the soup can, to lick my face and contented himself with cocking a convivial leg against the bottom step.

I stared into Mrs. Westby's radiant face. "What what . . . ?"

With her sparkling eyes and wide smile, she looked more attractive than ever. "Look, Mr. Herriot, look! He's better, he's better!"

In an instant I was wide awake. "And I . . . I suppose you'll want me to get that can off him?"

"Oh, yes, yes, please!"

It took all my strength to lift him onto the table. He was heavier now than before his illness. I reached for the familiar forceps and began to turn the jagged edges of the can outwards from the nose and mouth. Tomato soup must have been one of his favourites because he was really deeply embedded, and it took some time before I was able to slide the can from his face.

I fought off his slobbering attack. "He's back in the dustbins, I see."

"Yes, he is, quite regularly. I've pulled several cans off him myself. And he goes sliding with the children, too." She smiled happily.

Thoughtfully I took my stethoscope from the pocket of my white coat and listened to his lungs. They were wonderfully clear. A slight roughness here and there, but the old cacophony had gone.

I leaned on the table and looked at the great dog with a mixture of thankfulness and incredulity. He was as before, boisterous and full of the joy of living.

I leaned on the table and looked at the great dog with a mixture of thankfulness and incredulity. He was as before, boisterous and full of the joy of living. His tongue lolled in a happy grin, and the sun glinted through the surgery window on his sleek golden coat.

"But Mr. Herriot," Mrs. Westby's eyes were wide, "how on earth has this happened? How has he got better?"

"Vis medicatrix naturae," I replied in tones of deep respect.

"I beg your pardon?"

"The healing power of nature. Something no veterinary surgeon can compete with when it decides to act."

"I see. And you can never tell when this is going to happen?"

"No."

For a few seconds we were silent as we stroked the dog's head and ears and flanks.

"Oh, by the way," I said, "has he shown any renewed interest in the blue jeans?"

"Oh, my word, yes! They're in the washing machine at this very moment. Absolutely covered in mud. Isn't it marvellous!"

Above: *This two-month-old yellow Lab knows how to deal with the heat of summer.* Photo © Jack Macfarlane
Facing page: *The hunter's hand steadies a young Lab in the field.* Photo © Bill Buckley/The Green Agency
Overleaf: *"If the label 'workaholic' can be applied to a dog, it aptly fits the Lab."* John R. Falk, Gun Dogs, *1997. Photo* © William H. Mullins

Above: *Taking to the air to snag a bean bag, a Labrador pup gets some exercise in a Montana field.* Photo © Alan and Sandy Carey

Left: *"A dog who forgets that he is dealing with a mere human being is apt to expect too much of his man, and will be disappointed when the man fails to measure up to certain canine standards of intelligence." Corey Ford, "Every Dog Should Have a Man."* Photo © Bill Buckley/The Green Agency

Above: *"[The Labrador] has a form which can justly be called artistic and a range of colourings which affords a choice to those who wish to indulge their taste for tones that attest and delight the eye. The sheen of the coat is a great attraction and for those who are not attracted by the jet black of the more popular variety there is available the yellow Labrador, whose colouring may vary from the luxuriance of fox-red to the delicacy of cream."* Rowland Johns, Our Friend the Labrador, *1934.* Photo © William H. Mullins

Facing page: *A nine-month-old black Lab relaxes in the arms of its owner.* Photo © William H. Mullins

The general appearance of the Labrador should be that of a strongly built, short-coupled, very active dog. He should be fairly wide over the loins, and strong and muscular in the hindquarters. The coat should be close, short, dense and free from feather.
The American Kennel Club,
"The Official Standard for the Labrador Retriever,"
The Complete Dog Book, 1992

Above: *A chocolate Lab pup mugs for the camera with an equine friend.* Photo © Kent and Donna Dannen
Right: *The sun is just rising, but this hunting pair has already found success in the field. Despite the low light, the Lab retrieves the duck and returns to hand without difficulty.* Photo © William H. Mullins

If a man's dog leaves him, his time in this world is short.
—Folk saying from the Oklahoma Ozarks

All Ghosts Aren't White

by Mel Ellis

 When researching for a book on any subject related to the outdoors, the work of the late Mel Ellis constantly surfaces. The longtime outdoor writer for the *Milwaukee Journal* composed more than twenty books, and his articles and essays for the paper and other publications would likely circle Lake Michigan—if someone was motivated to lay them out side-by-side, of course. Three of his books found their way to the big screen, including *Wild Goose, Brother Goose,* a novel written from the viewpoint of Duke, a Canada goose.

But Ellis also wrote about dogs with passion—particularly gun dogs. This is the story of a "phantom" Labrador of the Great Lakes, a dog that achieved legendary status due to the cruelty of one man and the kindness of another.

Acclimated to water as a pup, this Lab has no qualms about wading up to its haunches in a reedy marsh. Photo © Lon E. Lauber

Big water with its weird white fronts of fog does things to men's minds, and forgotten tales sometimes take on substance away out where the gulls fly patrol. Perhaps that is why men on the ore boats that ply the Great Lakes docked with stories of a big black Labrador, with a duck between its jaws, swimming through the mists many miles from any shore.

Sober men might have wondered what sort of ration the oreboat men were being served if it had not been that others also claimed to have seen the dog. Duck hunters fought snow storms back to shore to tell of a huge black dog, its muzzle white with frost. Commercial fishermen untangling nets said they'd seen the Labrador swimming through heavy seas, and they all claimed the dog had a duck between its jaws.

It was eight years since the first fisherman docked at Wisconsin's Fish Creek Harbor in Green Bay to ask if anyone had lost a Labrador as "big as a Shetland pony and black as midnight." I was stowing gear aboard a big boat for an island hunt and walked over in the twilight to listen.

"He stood on the point of Treasure Island and he had a duck in his mouth," the fisherman said. "We whistled but he couldn't hear me on account of the roaring surf. Then we edged in as close to shore as we dared without going aground, but he ducked into the brush. And yet there were no duck hunters out there today."

The next morning I combed Treasure Island with a friend whose name must even remain a secret, we'll call him Jerry. Treasure is the largest of the Strawberry group. We found huge imprints in the sand where a dog had run the night before. Thinking that maybe the animal had crossed to another island, we spent most of the afternoon searching three rocky outcroppings nearby. We killed a limit of goldeneyes while doing so, but found no further trace of the dog.

In Milwaukee that night I looked in the classified advertisements—and there was an ad promising a reward for the return of a black Labrador "lost on the Strawberry Islands."

Next morning I phoned the man who had advertised and told him what I knew. For obvious reasons, I'm not going to reveal his name, but will identify him only as R.J.H.

"That's Jeff, all right," he declared. "I wouldn't give a penny reward for him if I didn't know a guy who'll buy him as soon as I can get a rope around his neck."

As I hung up the receiver I hoped R.J.H. wouldn't get his dog back. I didn't know exactly why I felt that way, but somehow he chilled me.

Next day I called Jerry. I started off by telling him about this R.J.H. who had lost his dog. "You haven't seen the Labrador, have you?"

"What did you say the man's name was?" Jerry asked.

I repeated the name. "Know him?"

There was a long silence. Finally Jerry said that he did, that he had guided for the man once, but that he'd never let him set foot on one of

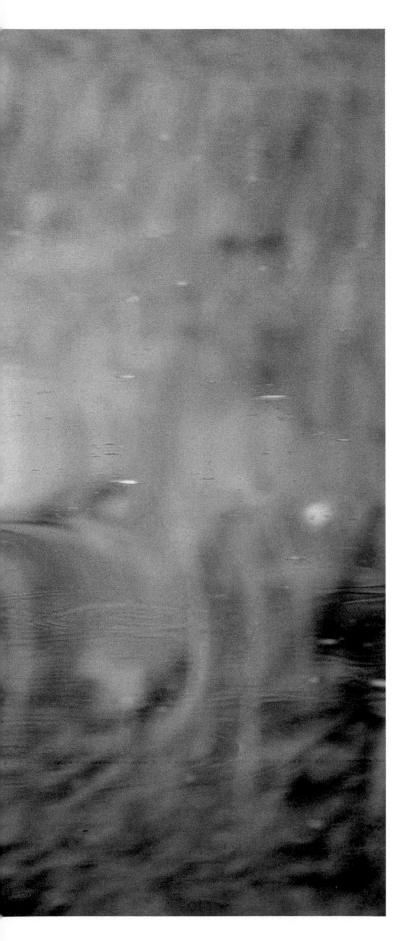

The Labrador's [coat] needed no reinforcement
and was already adapted to all extremes, the
flat, thick hairs so close together that they made
an almost waterproof surface.
Sheila Burnford, *The Incredible Journey*, 1971

*"The [Labrador retriever] may be known by having a close
coat which turns off water like oil . . ." The Third Earl of
Malmesbury.* Photo © Alan and Sandy Carey

his boats again. I wanted to go into it further, but long-distance telephone calls cost money, so I figured to take it up with Jerry the next time I saw him. After I'd hung up I remembered that Jerry had forgotten to say whether or not he'd seen the dog.

On a hunch, I phoned the editor of a field-trial publication. He knew the man and told me about him. Said that while judging a field trial he had disqualified the fellow for abusing his entry.

That afternoon I shot some pigeons for a retriever trainer named Chuck, who lived north of Milwaukee. He knew the man, too—had trained the dog for him. "And what a dog!" he said. "One of the most promising youngsters I've ever seen."

"What about the man?" I asked.

Chuck frowned and talked reluctantly. But between his story and the editor's I could piece the picture together. Evidently here was a dog completely loyal to a man who gave him nothing but abuse.

Chuck told me he'd asked the man to leave his place after he'd kicked the dog for failure to remain steady on the line. "But the dog stuck to him," Chuck said. "I've seldom seen retrievers take that sort of treatment and keep coming back for more. But that was the kind of dog Jeff was. Once he set out to do a thing, he stuck to it until it was done—whether it was making a retrieve, whipping another dog, or licking this guy's boots. You figure it."

I couldn't, so I forgot about it until about a week later, when the man who had lost the Lab called again. He wanted to know if I'd heard anything further. I told him I hadn't and—intrigued by now—asked him how he'd lost the dog.

"The fool went out after a goldeneye and just didn't come back," he said.

"Just didn't come back?" I repeated incredulously.

"That's what I said," R.J.H. replied. "The duck was a cripple and he followed it. I whistled, but he kept going."

"But," I said, "you went after him in a boat, didn't you?"

"Not on your life I didn't. It was blowing. I wasn't going to get wet. Water was coming over the gunwales and it was freezing."

"Oh," I said, and hung up.

I had the picture now, and it wasn't a pretty one. The man had been hunting a small island north of Treasure Island. The dog had never heard the whistle above the pounding surf. Intent on completing the retrieve, Jeff had become lost out among the big waves and eventually wound up on the wrong island.

I felt sure someone would pick up the dog, but three weeks later it was apparent that no one had, because the man called me again. "I think somebody is keeping my dog," he said.

"Maybe you're right," I agreed. "But how are you going to prove it?"

"Oh, I can prove it if I can locate the dog. I've got my initials R.J.H. tattooed in his left ear."

Winter came in quick that year. I didn't hear from R.J.H. again, but

the following spring and summer I heard rumors of a big black Labrador being sighted in the vicinity of the Strawberry Islands. It wasn't until fall, however, that an Associated Press story came across my desk quoting a commercial fisherman as saying he'd seen a Labrador as huge as a small horse on the shores of Treasure Island—a dog carrying a duck.

It was a good story as such stories go, but I threw it in the wastebasket. For one thing, I didn't want R.J.H. to read it. Not that I believed the fisherman, but some people might. And a good newspaper doesn't encourage the circulation of stories having no basis in fact.

Less than a week later one of our correspondents sent in another story telling how three duck hunters had seen the big black dog silhouetted against an early-morning moon on the rocky point of the

A black Lab wades ashore with a pintail. Photo © Gary Kramer island, staring out toward the open water. He was still carrying the duck.

This time I couldn't ignore the story. State papers were picking it up. Nobody believed it, but to them the apparition was symbolic of the perfect retriever roaming endlessly through a world of water and sky with no thought but to complete his retrieve.

That winter R.J.H. kicked one dog too many and was brought to court for cruelty to animals. This was the first time I'd got a look at him, and I didn't like what I saw. That made it still more difficult to understand how a dog could give so much love and loyalty to a man who deserved it so little.

I finally filed big Jeff's love for R.J.H. in the same pigeonhole in which would be filed the love story of a woman who follows a no-good husband straight through hell to be by his side. It was one of those things you don't figure out—just accept.

I wrote and told Jerry what had happened to R.J.H. A night or so later he phoned me and spent nearly $10.00 in toll charges telling me how he figured R.J.H. had got just what he deserved. That wasn't like Jerry, so I wondered after he'd hung up why he was so concerned over the fate of a man he guided but once.

For six years, then, the stories kept coming in. Sometimes bass fishermen would see the dog on a summer evening as they fished the reefs that ring the islands. The year the lake trout started to make a comeback, anglers bobbing through the ice told of a black dog trotting across the frozen horizon carrying a duck in its mouth.

. . . so how could I write about a scoundrel who'd abandon his dog to the elements? How could I write about a dog that had given his heart to a man who didn't deserve it?

It made intriguing copy unless you knew about R.J.H. and then it was kind of sickening. A score of times I was tempted to write the true story of how he'd deserted the dog. I figured the animal had starved the first winter, no dog could survive on those bleak islands. But when you're a newspaper man you never forget the law of libel, so how could I write about a scoundrel who'd abandon his dog to the elements? How could I write about a dog that had given his heart to a man who didn't deserve it?

I even searched for the animal's bones one spring while up bass fishing. But the islands have many bones of gulls and of crippled ducks that crawled ashore to die, of animals washed ashore, and even of Indians. I found no clue.

Several times I dropped off to see Jerry, but he was always out fishing. Then one fall there were no more stories about black ghost dogs, so I checked with Associated Press and they put a query on the

Facing page: Though Labs were first imported into the United States around the turn of the century, the first official American Kennel Club Lab arrived in 1917. Photo © Gary Kramer

wires. I called our correspondent on the lake front, and he talked with a score of duck hunters and commercial fishermen. But no one had seen the dog for nearly six months.

I supposed the story had just sort of worn itself out, that men had wearied of hearing it, and that those who visited the Strawberries didn't see the dog now because their imaginations had no news-story stimulation. In a way I was happy about it. It was one story I was content to let remain half written. I hadn't seen R.J.H. in years, and that was all right too.

I hadn't seen my friend Jerry either, and I was happy to get his call to come up to the islands for a hunt. "The goldeneyes are down this year, like they've never come through before," he said.

He knew that would get me. Shooting goldeneyes when they come whistling down from the Arctic with icicles goosing them all the way is a sport comparable to none. You hunt the big water and you fight ice on the decks, and waves coming over the gunwales, and snow in your eyes.

Jerry's dogs greeted me. There must have been six or eight in the kennel in back of the house, and they roared a welcome when I drove in. It was good seeing Jerry again after all those years. After dinner we sat in the living room, and it was then I noticed the big Labrador on the rug beside the chair.

"Going in for house dogs?" I asked.

Jerry laughed self-consciously. His wife had never let him bring a dog into the house. "This one is retired," he explained. "I retired him about six months ago."

Six months ago? I couldn't help remembering that it was just about six months ago that the last of the "Black Ghost" stories had come across my desk. I wondered. Jerry had retired lots of dogs in his time, but that hadn't meant they could come into the house to wait their lives out. I knew there was more.

"Good dog?" I asked.

"The best," Jerry said.

"Had him long?"

"Quite a while."

"Buy him from someone around here?"

Jerry nodded. "In a way you might say I did. Bought him, that is."

I leaned over then and flipped the Lab's left ear so that the initials R.J.H. were visible.

Jerry shifted uneasily in his chair. "To be honest with you—" he began.

"You don't have to honest with me," I interrupted. "Just tell me, when did you find him and did he still have the duck?"

Jerry walked over, knelt, and took the dog's graying muzzle between his hands. "I had him the very first night you called. I was about to tell you—I intended to tell you—but then you mentioned the name of the guy who'd lost him. I knew then I'd never tell anyone.

The Lab's tail beat a soft sound against the rug.

"Did he have the duck?" I asked.

"He had a duck. I don't know if it was the one he was chasing the

Labs are capable of some amazing feats; keep your keys in your pocket when your Lab has the run of the truck. Photo © Bill Buckley/The Green Agency

Above: *At first disdained by Labrador breeders, the chocolate Lab (the product of a variation of the yellow recessive gene) is preferred today by many show breeders.* Photo © Kent and Donna Dannen

Left: *It is not at all apparent that this yellow Lab mom realizes the gravity of the situation facing her.* Photo © Alan and Sandy Carey

day he got lost, or a cripple he'd picked up. You know how hard it is to kill goldeneyes. You know how the crips are always coming ashore in a blow. It might have been a crip."

"But—" Questions crowded to my mind. "How about the villagers, the hunters, the fishermen?"

Jerry scratched the dog's muzzle gently. "I knew they'd be looking for him. But I'd see Jeff dead before I'd let that louse get him back. So I locked him in my island fishing shack. He broke out a couple of times. Some of the oreboat deckhands and hunters must have seen him. Maybe he was even picking up cripples. I suppose that's how the stories got started. Then, just before the big freeze, I brought him home."

The big dog sighed. I sighed too, and as a man turns the page of a long, long book, I turned the big Lab's ear down to hide forever the initials R.J.H.

Above: *Lab puppies are notorious chewers. Your best defense is to keep anything you don't want chomped on out of reach and to provide their active mouths with plenty of expendable toys—such as this stick suitable for a party of three.* Photo © Alan and Sandy Carey

Facing page: *Labs are effective upland retrievers; this Lab carries a ruffed grouse.* Photo © Bill Marchel

Above: *A Lab pup, two and a half months old, rests in the backyard.* Photo © William H. Mullins
Facing page: *A black Lab adult and a yellow Lab pup sitting in the field.* Photo © Bruce
Montagne

Above: *"It was claimed for [Labrador retrievers] that their maritime existence [in Newfoundland], prolonged through countless ages, had resulted in webbed feet, a coat impervious to water like that of an otter, and a short, thick 'swordlike' tail, with which to steer safely their stoutly made frames amid the breakers of the ocean." Charles Eley,* The History of Retrievers, *1921.* Photo © Alan and Sandy Carey

Above: *Nothing pulls at the heartstrings like the innocent eyes of a Labrador pup.* Photo © William H. Mullins

Overleaf: *A gritty yellow Lab is up with the sun, ready for a day in the field.* Photo © Jack Macfarlane

*The great pleasure of a dog is that you may make a fool of yourself with him and
not only will he not scold you, but he will make a fool of himself too.*
—Samuel Butler

Tale *of the* Bewildered Bird Dog

by David Morine

David Morine served as The Nature Conservancy's Vice President of Land
Acquisition for more than eighteen years, work that resulted in the protec-
tion of two thousand significant natural areas totaling some three million
acres (1.2 million hectares). Now a freelance writer based in Virginia,
David has written two books, *Good Dirt: Confessions of a Conservationist* and *The Class
Choregus*. His writing has appeared in numerous publications, including *Field & Stream*,
American Forests, and *Down East*. He is in the process of writing a third book, and also assists
local land conservation groups with their land acquisition efforts.

"Tale of the Bewildered Bird Dog," which first appeared in *Sports Illustrated*, is the story
of one of David's diplomatic efforts to gain support for his land acquisition work in Texas. As
it turns out, David quickly discovers that the fastest way to win over a certain influential
Texan was to make friends with his Lab.

A content chocolate Lab waits patiently by the side of a marsh. Photo © William H. Mullins

IN THE MID-'70s, The Nature Conservancy planned to start a major program in Texas. I was director of The Conservancy's land acquisition staff in those days, and we realized that setting aside acreage in Texas was not going to be easy. Residents of the former Republic of Texas don't appreciate anybody telling them what to do with their land.

The strategy we decided to use to get the program started was to find a single influential Texan and sell him on our brand of conservation, rather than a general solicitation drive among owners of desirable sites. As land-acquisition director, it was my task to find that Texan.

It took me only a few phone calls to identify the person we wanted. He was big, even by Texas standards. He had inherited one fortune and made another. He supported habitat-preservation organizations like Ducks Unlimited, Boone and Crockett Club, and Safari Club International. Apparently nothing concerning conservation in Texas was undertaken without his approval. He was not a member of The Nature Conservancy.

When I called him, he seemed receptive. In fact, he invited me to go hunting. "Come down after the first of the year and we'll get some snows," he said. "Provided you ain't opposed to hunting?" He was testing me, obviously.

"That would be fine," I told him. "I enjoy hunting." Which was the truth. I did enjoy the one time in my life that I went hunting. Professional conservationists do not get many invitations to go hunting.

"Good. We'll go up to Eagle Lake," the Texan said. "Goose capital of the world. You've never seen anything like it."

Right after the New Year, I flew to Houston. Eagle Lake was about 50 miles west. My Texan met me at the airport. For the sake of this story, and my health, let's say he went by the initials, T.H. He was wearing big boots, a big hat and a big belt buckle and was smoking the biggest cigar I had ever seen. His big four-wheel drive was parked right

in front of the door. It was filled to the roof with camouflage clothes, gun cases, boxes of shells and racks of decoys. A dog cage was nestled in the middle. Its door was open.

A black Lab retrieves a snow goose through decoys strewn about a grain field. Photo © Bill Marchel

As soon as I got in, a young, enthusiastic Lab jumped into my lap and started licking my face. "That's Lieutenant Colonel William Barret Travis," T.H. told me. "I'm just breaking him in. I had his daddy for 12 years. Best retriever in all of Texas. I had to put him down last year, but this here dog, he's going to be even better." T.H. must truly have high hopes for this dog, I thought. Lt. Col. William Barret Travis commanded the Alamo, and his name is not bestowed casually in the state of Texas.

"Remember the Alamo!" I said, scratching Trav's ears. "You can't beat a good dog."

"Ain't that the truth," T.H. said. He floored the big vehicle, cut off a taxi and barreled out of the airport.

As we rambled through mile after mile of south Texas ranchland, I tried to steer the conversation toward conservation, but T.H. didn't want to talk about conservation. He wanted to talk about Travis. "Ol' Trav here, he's going to be a champ," T.H. said. "Smart as a whip, and there's nothing he can't find." According to T.H., Travis had the best nose, most brains, softest mouth and biggest heart of any dog in all of Texas.

"Good boy, Trav," I said, wiping a glob of drool off my blazer. It didn't take me 50 miles to figure out that being nice to Lt. Col. Travis would help me get a program going in Texas.

A black Lab wades through a marsh with a firm hold on a snow goose. Photo © Bill Marchel

We pulled into Eagle Lake at dusk. It was, in fact, a one-horse town—there was a single hitching post in front of The Farris 1912. In its brochure, The Farris 1912 described itself as "A Step Back in Time . . . the Queen of Early Texas Hotels." As we walked in, men in big boots, big hats and big belt buckles were sitting around, smoking big cigars. As far as I could tell, there were no women registered at The Farris 1912.

My Texan knew everyone. After a big country dinner, we settled into one of The Farris 1912's public lounges for some big drinks and some big Texas stories. Every story revolved around hunting. When they started comparing dogs, T.H. rambled on and on about Travis. "T.H., that dog's just a pup," noted a little Texan, who may have been trying to compensate for his size by the very big diamond ring on his pinkie. "Now his daddy, he was a retriever, but this dog hasn't shown us anything yet." The other men at The Farris 1912 agreed.

"You'll be believers by this time tomorrow," T.H. said as he stomped off to bed. Beautiful! This slight to Trav was the chance I'd been looking for. If I could help make the pup a star, we'd be set in Texas. I tossed down another big drink to celebrate my good luck. Now all I had to do was prove myself in the field.

It was 4:30 a.m. when we piled into the truck. There was no sign of daylight. I hadn't been able to eat my big country breakfast. My head was killing me from all the big drinks. Luckily, I'd remembered Travis and had stuffed my pockets with patties of spicy breakfast sausage.

We rattled through the darkness over gravel roads, splashing through puddles and potholes. "This land used to be the Garwood and Eagle Lake prairies," T.H. told me. He seemed to be in a better mood now that we had gotten away from The Farris 1912 and the little man with the big diamond pinkie ring.

The smell of Travis's sausage-scented breath as he continually lapped my cheek was getting to me. Thanks to the sausage, Travis was becoming my best friend.

"In the late '40s and early '50s, Jimmy Reel, a rice buyer and a helluva hunter from Arkansas, convinced these landowners to spot their rice fields with ponds," he said, slamming the gears into four-wheel drive as we skidded onto a dirt track. Travis was crawling all over me, trying to get at the spicy sausage. "Jimmy figured if we had some water, all this rice would attract a lot of geese," T.H. continued. "He was right. Within 10 years, a million snows were wintering over, and Eagle Lake was calling itself the undisputed goose-hunting capital of the world."

"Interesting," I said, surreptitiously slipping Travis a sausage patty. I was having trouble concentrating on the history of the Garwood and Eagle Lake prairies. The smell of Travis's sausage-scented breath as he continually lapped my cheek was getting to me. Thanks to the sausage, Travis was becoming my best friend.

A faint glow was spreading from the east as we slid to a stop. T.H. dropped the tailgate and hauled out a huge sack and two gun cases. "You grab the guns, and I'll take the gear," he said, slinging the sack over his shoulder. "All right, Trav, it's time to show those boys back at The Farris who's boss." Travis ignored T.H. and stuck his nose under my down vest. "I can't believe it," said T.H. "Travis's taking to a conservationist. That's like licking Santa Anna."

We started to slosh through the rice furrows. A couple of inches of standing water separated each row from the next. Gobs of mud clung to my boots. My feet felt as heavy as cinder blocks.

We stopped next to a pond. The day was arriving overcast and unseasonably hot. I put down the gun cases and unzipped my vest. The rice fields stretched to the horizon in every direction. I was about to collapse when T.H. said, "We'll set up here. That way, we might get some ducks coming into the pond as well as geese feeding in the field. Travis likes them both. That's right, isn't it, boy?"

Travis didn't hear him. Or at least he didn't pay him any attention. He was too busy sniffing my pockets searching for more spicy sausage. When T.H. wasn't looking, I gave Travis another patty. It was gone in a single gulp.

T.H. dumped his bag on the ground. Much to my surprise, he pulled out two long, white surgical gowns and a big pile of diapers. "Here, put this on," he said, handing me one of the gowns. He had to be putting me on. Where was the traditional camouflage?

He put on his gown and picked up an armload of diapers.

"Diapers? What are they for?" I asked.

"Decoys," he said. "Ain't nothing that decoys snows better than diapers."

This was unbelievable. Diapers for decoys, white gowns as camouflage. T.H. had to be kidding.

He was dead serious. "Follow me and spread these out," he ordered. "The geese are going to be in the air right quick, and we're going to knock down a bunch of them. Those boys back at The Farris are going to be eating their words tonight." T.H. started dropping diapers in the field. I squished after him.

Spreading the diapers was no easy job. There were hundreds of them. Sweat fogged my glasses and dripped off my nose. I kept tripping over my gown. My legs felt like jelly. Travis kept hounding me for more spicy sausage. "Daggone," said T.H., "I've never seen a dog take to anybody like that. I patted Travis on the head and snuck him another patty. He swallowed it and stared at me, begging for more.

I was so exhausted that it took me a moment to hear the honking. Geese, thousands of them, were getting up. A solid wall of birds was forming like a cloud. It began rolling over the rice fields toward us. "Let's go!" hollered T.H. He threw down the last of his diapers and sprinted back to where we had left the guns. I stood there, numbed by the sight. I'd never seen so many birds. "Come on!" T.H. shouted. A rush of adrenaline gave me a second wind. I plowed through the furrows after him.

Above: *Taking to the air, a black Lab launches from a bank in pursuit of a retrieve.* Photo © Bill Buckley/ The Green Agency
Facing page: *A young Lab sharpens his teeth on a sapling.* Photo © William H. Mullins

"Here," T. H. said, unlatching the gun cases and handing me a beautiful over-and-under. "You shoot the 12. I'll shoot my 10." His 10-gauge was the biggest gun I had ever seen. It looked like a cannon. "I'll tell you when to shoot. First bird's yours."

I lay down and loaded my gun. T.H. and Travis nestled in behind me. The geese now had Travis's full attention. He had forgotten all about the spicy sausage. His mind was riveted on retrieving.

T.H. produced a goose call and started honking. A couple of dozen birds immediately peeled off from the main flock and were decoyed right to the diapers. Travis whimpered as he watched them coming in. "Steady, boy, steady," T.H. softly crooned. Honk! Honk! Honk! "Steady." Honk! Honk! The geese circled in right on top of us. "Now," T. H. said.

I sat up, took aim, and pulled the trigger. Nothing happened. "Damn," I said, fumbling with the safety.

Travis ignored his master. He splashed across the furrows, trustingly expecting a bird to fall. He must have run half a mile before he stopped and watched the geese fly out of sight. I could see he was confused. Why hadn't any fallen?

"Shoot! Shoot!" yelled T.H. The flock wheeled and flew off across the fields. I clicked off the safety, raised my gun and fired. At the sound, Travis burst past me. "Whoa! Whoa!" screamed T.H., knowing that the geese had far outdistanced the pellets I had sent their way. Travis ignored his master. He splashed across the furrows, trustingly expecting a bird to fall. He must have run half a mile before he stopped and watched the geese fly out of sight. I could see he was confused. Why hadn't any fallen?

T.H. was red-faced from blowing his dog call. "Back, Travis, back!" he hollered. "Back, boy!" He whistled some more. When Travis finally returned, he was caked with mud. Saliva foamed in his otherwise empty mouth. He didn't look like much of a star. He flopped into my lap, obviously expecting at least one patty for all of his effort. "Damn. That dog has got a big heart," T.H. marveled. "I'd of bit you if you had done that to me."

"I got mixed up with the safety," I apologized. "I've never shot this type of gun before."

"Never mind," T.H. said, scanning the sky. "Quick, get down. Here come some teal."

I looked up and watched a flock of blue-winged teal drop from the sky and sweep in low over the pond. They were wingtip-to-wingtip. It was like watching a precision flying team. "Shoot! Dammit, shoot!" hollered T.H. I rolled up to a sitting position and fired wildly into the formation. Travis was off at the flash. He plunged into the pond. I prayed at least one bird would fall. None did.

T.H. pulled out his recall whistle again. Tweet! Tweet! "Back, Travis! Back!" Tweet! Tweet! Travis paddled on, unmindful of T.H.'s frantic calls. He wasn't about to surrender. Lieutenant Colonel William B. would have been proud of his namesake. "There's no bird, daggone it!" screamed T.H.

"Travis! Come back, boy! The damn Yankee missed again!"

Travis's tongue was dragging as he struggled up the bank. It had been a long swim. He stopped next to me, shook himself and plopped his head into my lap. Surely, there'd be a treat this time.

"I swear, I can't believe this," said T.H., looking at his ever-forgiving retriever.

"These birds fly faster than the ones I'm used to," I said lamely. "I

Two yellow Lab pups wade in the beachfront shallows. Photo © Tara Darling

haven't been leading them enough." My explanation was for the birds, and T.H. knew it.

"Get set," he said. "Here come some more geese." Honk! Honk! Travis looked up and started to whine. The sky was white with geese. Even I couldn't miss.

BOOOOM! I was so startled by the sound of the 10-gauge that I dropped my gun. Two geese immediately folded and tumbled to the ground. I could see T.H.'s hubris settle as Travis instinctively marked

Above: *A yellow and a black Lab cool off on a hot summer day.* Photo © Jim Schlender

Facing page: *Give this Lab a rifle and the owner wouldn't even need to go along on the hunt.* Photo © Bill Buckley/The Green Agency

both birds. He fetched one, then flawlessly went back and picked up the other. It was a perfect retrieve, one that had all the markings of a great story.

T.H. beamed with pride as Travis pranced past me with the second bird. Travis didn't even give me a glance. My spicy sausage couldn't compete with the natural taste of warm goose. This dog was a born retriever, a guaranteed star.

"I'm sorry, son," T.H. said, removing the second bird from Travis's mouth. "But I had to shoot. You were wrecking my dog."

I've never been back to Texas. After my trip to Eagle Lake, The Nature Conservancy hired someone specifically to run our Texas program. He was a crack shot and did an outstanding job selling The Conservancy's brand of conservation to the sportsmen of Texas. He told me they remember me at The Farris 1912; that I play a lead role in one of T.H.'s best "dawg" stories. T.H. can't figure out what Travis ever saw in me. Maybe someday I'll call him and tell him about the sausage. It will add spice to his story.

Above: *Taking a water break at a show.* Photo © Tara Darling
Facing page: *A Lab bolts into a bay at the signal from its owner.* Photo ©
Gary Kramer

Above: *A chocolate Lab puppy on a sunny day in the Rocky Mountain foothills.* Photo © Kent and Donna Dannen
Facing page: *"I have long been land-poor for the simple reason that I keep Labrador retrievers." Gene Hill,* Tears and Laughter, *1981.* Photo © William H. Mullins

Above: *It's relaxation time for this yellow Lab and its owner.* Photo © Bill Buckley/The Green Agency
Right: *A black Lab leaps into a marsh to retrieve a downed duck.* Photo © Bill Marchel

The sound of a shot and the splash of a duck had had the same effect on the Labrador as a trumpet call to an old war horse, and drew him as irresistibly. Without a second's hesitation he had plunged in for the retrieve, only to find that he was unable to open his mouth to grasp the heavy duck properly, and was forced to tow it ashore by a wingtip. He emerged from the water twenty feet from the man, the beautiful greenhead trailing from its outstretched wing, the sun striking the iridescent plumage. The Labrador looked doubtfully at the stranger, and Mackenzie stared back in open-mouthed amazement. For a moment the two were frozen in a silent tableau . . .
—Sheila Burnford, *The Incredible Journey*, 1971

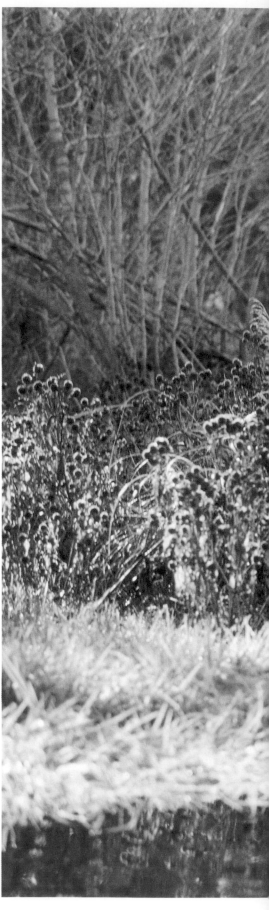

Above: *A yellow Lab returns a duck to hand.* Photo © Bruce Montagne
Right: *Not needing binoculars, two chocolate Labs scan the skies with their owner.* Photo © Alan and Sandy Carey

Above all, there are [my Lab Gypsy's] eyes. It is a wonderful thing when a dog speaks to a man with her eyes. . . . Gypsy has yet more to tell than she knows now, she is so young. She sits at my feet, and I know what she is going to do; she suddenly stands on her hind feet, puts her paws on my shoulder and looks at me long and long. Some day, perhaps, I shall know it all, but to-day she is still learning, still trying to understand and tell me more. And she does tell me more, as the years grow with her, and for that I thank the world that gave her to me.
—Eric Parker, *Best of Dogs*, 1949

One

by Gene Hill

Gene Hill is as comfortable as old hunting boots, a relaxing storyteller fitting for a cold winter night spent deep in a favorite chair near the hearth. He is a most human hunter and writes with humility of his often less-than-successful trips afield. Through his struggles, his readers can see themselves.

As a longtime contributing editor to *Field & Stream*, his monthly "Hill Country" column reaches a wide audience. He is the author of many books, including *A Hunter's Fireside Book*, *Mostly Tailfeathers*, *A Listening Walk . . . and Other Stories*, and *Tears and Laughter: A Couple of Dozen Dog Stories*.

Gene Hill is also a Labrador owner, and stories about the breed appear frequently in his writing. Whether it is puppies chewing up his favorite shoes, a field-trial champion pursuing a double retrieve, or an old, tired Lab sleeping on the rug, there always seems to be a Labrador underfoot. This story from *Tears and Laughter* relates the painful tale of a remarkable dog. But it's also the story of a remarkable man, whose priorities evolve as the story of "One" unfolds.

"'Almost everyone was soon calling him One, short for number one because that's what he looked like right from the start.'" Photo © Lon E. Lauber

I ADMIRED THE dog out of courtesy and that was about it. He wasn't anything special to look at—just your nice, solid, big-headed black Lab. I've seen hundreds just like him, give or take an inch here or a detail there. His work in the field was efficient, but not exciting. He wasn't what a real trial man would call steady and as often as not he'd drop a goose to readjust a hold; generally preferring to drag it along by a wing. He did have one peculiar habit I noticed—he never picked up a bird, no matter how dead it was without stepping on the neck with one foot first and holding it there until he'd grabbed the wing. I asked about this, and his owner told me that it was a habit he'd had from the first, since his first goose had picked him pretty bad. This bit of cause and effect reasoning pleased me being a "once burned, twice shy" person myself.

This day in a goose pit on the eastern shore of Maryland was as common as the surrounding mud. Intermittent flights had us calling, more for the amusement of it than any real hope of turning them. But every so often a pair or a small flock of five or six would toll close enough for a shot and since we were in no hurry or that anxious to take geese, we took turns gunning. By mid-afternoon we each had two geese—enough for our personal satisfaction, but the weather was mild so we had come to a mutual unspoken agreement to just sit there and chat rather than pick up and go our seperate ways. It was a lovely way to spend an afternoon—gunning talk mostly, a little fishing talk, some book titles exchanged—just your average small talk between two relative strangers who found common ground and an occasional bit of laughter that sweetened the conversation putting each of us at ease and wanting the other to find us good company . . . a small, pleasant spontaneous friendship.

He hardly mentioned his Lab, and neither did I, but I was pleased to notice that the dog sat leaning a little against his masters leg or put his head on his foot when he chose to lie down, and that my companion's hand was stroking the dog or messing with his ears or scratching him behind the neck. It was just the sort of thing any one of us might do, an ordinary circumstance, a commonplace relationship. Nor did I find it strange that the dog paid absolutely no attention to me whatsoever. There are dogs that are nuisances for affection (several of mine were like that from being spoiled and encouraged to play) and others that like to keep to themselves, and others that are clearly one person creatures.

He had not bothered to bring a lunch, and I, for once, had gotten myself together and packed one. As usual, when I do get the lunch-making urge, I tend to go overboard and had more than enough to share, which I gladly did. We each had two sandwiches, and as he ate his he fed the other to his dog at the

Below: *A Labrador is a powerful swimmer, and its tail acts as a rudder when the dog takes to the water.*
Photo © Bill Marchel
Facing page: *A brown-eyed black Lab waits near the edge of a pond.*
Photo © William H. Mullins

same pace, bite for bite. A sandwich and a half was enough for me, so I offered the dog the half left over. He wouldn't touch it from my hand, so I placed it on the floor of the blind in front of him where it sat unnoticed and untasted until I asked my friend if the dog were on some sort of self-imposed diet.

"No, I don't think so," he laughed, and picked up the food and as before fed it to the dog bite by bite.

You can usually sense when someone has been waiting for a chance to talk about something that needs to be aired. You feel that he's been looking for the right time and place and ear. I was hoping that I'd have that privilege, so I just sat there and watched him dribble pieces of that sandwich, pieces about the size of 00 Buck, to a dog that was not only used to this little game, but so delighted with it that he was making soft moaning noises and rolling his eyes like a fundamentalist convert.

"Pete, here, is about the worst dog I've ever owned," he said with some hesitation, "but he's taught me more about dogs, in a strange way, than most of the others I've had—and there have been quite a few."

I just sat there and stared at the floor of the blind, not wanting to look at him, because he didn't want to look at me . . . right now he wanted a listener, a sympathetic and understanding one—one who had some knowledge of what he was talking about, but not a conversation—just the ear would do fine for the time being.

"If you've ever followed the big field trial circuit you'd probably know my name. For quite a few years I was the amateur trainer that most of the pro's worried about. And they had good reason. I had the money, the time, the drive and the dogs. And you needed all that just to start because you were in against the Belmonts, the Roosevelts, big steel money, big oil money and just plain money so big that hardly anyone remembered where it all had come from. One handler drove his dogs to the trials in an old Rolls Royce fitted up like a kennel truck; the people he worked for drove Rolls' and they didn't want their dogs in anything less! I didn't go that far . . . but I wasn't too far behind. I've charted more than one plane to take my dogs where I thought they ought to be running and I never regretted a penny of it.

"I even had Purdey make me a pair of side-bys just for field trial gunning in case my dogs didn't finish so I'd still be part of the action— and you learn a lot about certain dogs when you're a gun—but that's getting a little away from my story.

"It all started simply enough—and typically as far as I'm concerned. I've always loved competition—I've been a top flight amateur golfer, a tournament winner on the trap and skeet circuit, and got to where they knew I was there in the live bird rings of Madrid and Monte Carlo. Then I got to thinking about getting a dog. I traveled so much in my early days that owning one didn't make much sense. My hosts, when I went shooting, all had fine kennels so it didn't make any difference if I had any or not. In fact it was better that I didn't. But when a big holding company bought me out for more money than I could ever spend and moved me up to some spot that was all title and no work, I began to look around for something new to take up. It was just about destined that I'd start field trialing Labs.

"I'd been a member of one of those fancy Long Island duck clubs for years and had seen some pretty good dogs. It might sound silly, but I believe that a man has to have a dog and a breed of dog that suits his personality. If I believed in reincarnation I don't doubt that I'd come back as a Lab—or would like to. It's a little vain I know, but I saw myself as brave, honest and strong, as Hemingway might have put it, and that's what I like about the Lab. It's all up front, nothing held back.

"It's a little vain I know, but I saw myself as brave, honest and strong, as Hemingway might have put it, and that's what I like about the Lab. It's all up front, nothing held back."

"Anyway, one of my duck hunting buddies at the old Sprig Club had a litter of dogs out of good field trial stock and he gave me a male as sort of a retirement present. He said that at worst he'd be somebody I could talk to and take care of and get the same in return. After I'd spent a few weeks with the pup I decided to have a professional take a look at him. I felt that he might have what it would take to be a trial dog, but I believe in the opinions of the people who do it everyday, not just an amateur appraisal.

"The professional not only liked the dog but made an offer then and there to take him for training, and I agreed. He had a fine reputation and I liked his whole approach to the training idea. He was to start the dog, and when he was satisfied I'd come down and spend a week or so with him and learn to run the dog myself. Then I'd get a training schedule to work on and check back with him for a few days on a regular basis. If the dog did exceptionally well, he'd take him over completely and campaign in the major stakes. His name was Wonderdog—because I wondered what I'd do with him when I first got him; a little joke with myself. If you follow the retrievers you know how far he got and what a piece of pure bad luck it was he didn't become National Champion. He was killed a little while after his first Nationals—an assistant trainer was in an accident and the dog trailer was totally demolished. I was hurt by the loss, of course, but by then I'd been committed to try for another dog as good as he was. He'd sired a litter and I arranged to get the pick for stud service.

"If anything, he was better than his father; a bit more aggressive and strangely a bit more biddable. It was almost as if he felt destined to compete and understood what was expected of him all along. I called him Little Wonder—another private joke with myself. Almost everyone was soon calling him One, short for number one because that's what he

Though the breed as we know it today was developed in England, Labradors most likely originated in Newfoundland, along the Atlantic coast of Canada. Photo © William H. Mullins

looked like right from the start. He was one of the hottest derby dogs anyone had seen when he was right, and he usually was. I'd never thought of a dog as an athlete before One, but when he took to water he reminded me of a diver—I know it's silly to think of a dog having "form" but he did—and I never got over the idea that he knew it and worked at it.

"By the time he was three, One had totally captivated the trial circuit—not just in wins and placements, but by his personality—his pure competitiveness and genius for doing just the right thing at the right time. I know for sure that more than one judge laid out a series with just him in mind, but as hard as they tried to challenge him he was usually up to it. Of course he had an off-day now and then, disinterested or bored or maybe tired, but even then he did his job, but without the fire he was famous for. In his first National at Bombay Hook he placed third. I don't think he deserved to win, but I think he deserved at least second. The head judge and I weren't exactly friends, since I'd beaten his dog at several important trials and he wasn't above playing a little politics with some nationally known names.

"I'd planned to retire One after his first in the Nationals, and just use him as a stud dog and gunning companion. We'd become pretty close and I thought he deserved a little rest and some fun—and some of the fun had gone out of the competition as far as I was concerned. But I did want that win for him in the worst way. He'd worked hard for it and most of us still believed that he had the class and the talent to go all the way; if any dog deserved it, One certainly did. The more we worked him that season the sharper he got. I didn't think that there was much room for improvement, but in subtle ways he just looked better. His long blinds were precision itself and when he was stopped to the whistle he really *stopped*. It was as if he were reading your mind—I heard one judge remark in a friendly way that he looked as if he were showing off. I'm making him sound as if he were absolutely perfect, but he did have one small fault. Not in every trial, but every now and then for some reason he'd make one or two little yelps on a retrieve on land. I always put it down as pure enthusiasm and the trainer and I had long given up trying to make him stop. More often than not, we'd be the only ones to notice it."

Here he paused for so long I didn't think he was going to go on with the rest of the story. He was rumpling his dog and searching for the right words and the strength to say them. I had the feeling that this was a story that he'd never told before and perhaps didn't want to—yet knew that he must so he could get a different grip on it himself. For some strange reason I thought of the words to an old song about "hanging your tears out to dry"—how perfectly put, how perfectly true.

For the first time since he'd begun, he turned to look at me and I could see the gray, sad sparkle of small tears. I turned away a bit to give him a moment of privacy. He covered his face with his handkerchief for just a second and went on.

The snowcover is no deterrent whatsoever to this pheasant-retrieving chocolate Lab. Photo © Gary Kramer

"I'd say the chances of what happened ever happening are more than one in a million. One of those random tragedies that always seem to strike the innocent; the casual passerby. There was a strand of wire, just one, that was only about two feet long between an old post and a tree. I'd heard One making his odd yipping noise and suddenly he went end over end in the air and lay still. Both the judges and I rushed out knowing instantly that something fearful had happened, and there was One stretched out, dead from a broken neck. A small trickle of blood ran down the corners of his jaw where he'd run into the wire with his mouth open.

"I carried him back to the station wagon and put him on the front seat and started to drive. I don't remember how long it was or where I went, but I do remember that I kept rubbing his head believing for the longest time that he'd suddenly sit up and everything would be all right. Today is the second time in my life that I've cried; that was the first.

"Funny, isn't it, how few can understand the relationship a man can have with his dog? And yet, I can tell you now that there were few, if any, things in my life that meant as much to me as One, and how odd but true that an emptiness like that is there forever."

"There's a small graveyard behind the lodge at the Sprig Club where our special dogs were put to rest and the whole club turned out to help me put him there. I had a blanket made of his ribbons and my gunning coat was his pillow. He always loved to sleep on that whenever he had the chance. One of the members read a list of his wins and when finished with that, he paused, and in a soft tenor began to sing Auld Lang Syne and everyone, except me, joined in with him."

He stopped again for a minute and blew his nose; I must confess I did the same.

"I virtually stopped gunning for a long time after that. When people asked me why, I told them that my favorite partner had passed away and almost none of them ever thought that it might have been just my dog. Funny, isn't it, how few can understand the relationship a man can have with his dog? And yet, I can tell you now that there were few, if any, things in my life that meant as much to me as One, and how odd but true that an emptiness like that is there forever.

"It's been about five years since I lost One and last fall a friend of mine, the same one that sang that afternoon at the duck club, came to my house and rang the bell. When I opened the door he reached in and put a puppy in my arms and said, 'It's about time Pete had someone to look after,' and turned and left."

"This is Pete." At the sound of his name Pete looked up and made

A yellow Lab waits for the signal to retrieve. Photo © Alan and Sandy Carey

some sort of a face that I'll say was as close to smiling as a dog can get.

"When I said that Pete was the worst of my dogs I didn't mean anything but that I'd never trained him. I just let him be Pete. And that's been enough, more than enough. They say that a man deserves one good dog in his life . . . but that's not true. I've had a couple, and in his own way, Pete's right there in my heart with them all now. It's a full space with two empty ones beside it if you can see it that way."

I nodded to let him know that I agreed, but I didn't say anything because I didn't think anything needed to be said just at that moment.

He began, after a little while, to talk about something else and after giving me his card he thanked me for listening and said it was time for him and Pete to be heading on home. I said goodbye and told him that I'd wait here a little while longer in the blind just to watch the sun come down. But that wasn't the whole truth. What I wanted to do was sit there in the quiet of twilight and hear the soft phrases of that ancient Scottish melody again in my mind and picture the scene of that group of men singing a dog to eternity and comforting themselves in the timeless ritual of shared sorrow and the understanding of loss.

In the last light, I slung my two geese over my shoulder and started back to where I'd left the car. I found myself softly singing what I could remember of One's funeral song, and surprisingly, I wasn't as saddened by the idea as you'd imagine. The saving thought was one of remembrance; as long as a man lives, so will his dogs in one form or another . . . in a story or a song. One will always be there to take care of the other and I can't think of a nicer way to put it than we will "share a cup of kindness now . . ."

A black Lab lounges while waiting for his fishing companions to set sail. Photo © William H. Mullins

Above: *A Lab looks skyward at a passing flock of Canada geese.* Photo ©
Bill Buckley/The Green Agency

Left: *A black Lab retrieves a blue goose through the colorful reeds of a northern marsh.* Photo © Bill Marchel

Above: *A long day at the office for this pair of pups; they are too tired even for dinner!* Photo © Kent and Donna Dannen

Facing page: *Positioning itself for the best possible view, this yellow Lab checks out the scene from the back of a pickup.* Photo © Gary Kramer

Brothers and sisters, I bid you beware
Of giving your heart to a dog to tear.
Rudyard Kipling

Above: *A black Lab pup in a field of Colorado wildflowers.* Photo © Kent and Donna Dannen
Facing page: *A Minnesota Lab poses with a pintail drake.* Photo © Bill Marchel

From her earliest puppy days, [my Lab] would prick her ears and look about her at the sound of a gun. She will watch an aeroplane right across the sky, and if it fell, I feel that she would gallop to its fall to bring it to me.

Eric Parker, *Best of Dogs,* 1949

Above: *Yellow Labs napping in a body-heat-conserving pile of pups.* Photo © Alan and Sandy Carey
Facing page: *A chocolate Lab with golden eyes pauses in an autumn field.* Photo © Alan and Sandy Carey

*I firmly believe that some dogs can read minds. Dixie, my Labrador,
usually joins me at breakfast, and I usually give her a scrap of toast or bacon. I
have often noticed that when I decide to choose a scrap for her, and well before I
pick it up, she will trot to my side and stand, waiting. She must have read my
mind. There's no other plausible explanation.*

J. Bryan, III, *Hodgepodge II,* 1990

Bess' Story

by John Madson

John Madson wrote prolifically about the outdoors in publications as wide-ranging as *Audubon, National Geographic, Reader's Digest,* and *Smithsonian.* The author of several books, including *Stories From Under the Sky, Out Home, Where the Sky Began, Up on the River,* and *Tallgrass Prairie,* Madson was most comfortable in the natural world. He pursued his passion through his work as a wildlife biologist, naturalist, and writer. He wrote fulltime from 1980 until his death in 1995.

This is the story of Bess, a Labrador that seemingly does the impossible in a duck blind. This piece, arguably more than any other, gets closest to the true nature of the Labrador retriever. "Bess' Story" will amaze you at first, but in the end, you will know she had it in her all along. After all, she was a Lab.

Below: *Two pups small enough to be harassed by your average-sized dachshund pose for the camera.*
Photo © Tara Darling
Facing page: *In the earliest known reference to the Labrador breed, Colonel Peter Hawker, in* Instructions to Young Sportsman in all that Relates to the Guns and Shooting, *1814, wrote: "[The Labrador retriever], by far the best for every kind of shooting, is oftener* black *than of other colour, and scarcely bigger than a pointer. He is made rather long in the head and the nose; pretty deep in the chest; very fine in the legs; has* short *or* smooth *hair; does not carry his tail so much curled as [the Newfoundland]; and is extremely quick and active in running, swimming and fighting. . . ."*
Photo © William H. Mullins

LARRY REID STOPPED by awhile back, as he often does when he's got a new duck call. A new old one, I mean. He's afflicted with galloping collectivitis for vintage wildfowl calls, which isn't a bad way to go considering that they tend to appreciate in value, take up less room than a decoy collection, and never need dusting. Wives notice things like that—and a duck hunter can do with all the wifely goodwill he can get.

Settling down in my boar's nest of an office, Larry led me through the labyrinth of events that had resulted in his most recent acquisition—a battered walnut tube that was highballing mallards when Harding was president. The account of this odyssey lasted nearly as long as Harding's term of office.

At last the yarn was spun, the antique duck call slathered with praise, and a reflective pause entered the proceedings.

At last the yarn was spun, the antique duck call slathered with praise, and a reflective pause entered the proceedings.

"Reid," I observed, "for you, duck hunting is just an excuse to hunt junker duck calls."

"That is base calumny," he replied stiffly. "There's nothing I'd rather hunt than ducks. Especially when there's a bonus."

"Like another old duck call?"

"No, better than that . . ."

And away he went, again.

When things are right, the Batchtown Flats are a glory hole. A broad embayment of the Mississippi behind the Winfield Dam in southwestern Illinois, it's a thousand-acre duck haven of smartweed, millet, mudflats, and open shallows.

On that November day, though, things were not right. Comes to that, things couldn't have been much worse. Bluebird weather—clear, warm, quiet. The kind of day when Batchtown hunters have been known to fish for crappies from their blinds. At the Batchtown check station, there had been a wishful rumor that a new flight of ducks was on its way—but no one put much stock in that. Not with the forecast of a day in the balmy 60s with no weather fronts up north to push anything southward.

But you go hunting when you can, and Larry and his gunning partner, veterinarian Art Lippoldt, figured that hanging around a duck marsh beats hanging around town. Which, of course, it always does.

And so they headed out to their blind on Turner Island, a maze of

Above: *Full-speed ahead for this Lab retrieving a downed duck.* Photo © Lon E. Lauber
Right: *Watching and waiting for the ducks to come.* Photo © Alan and Sandy Carey

Above: *A yellow Lab retrieves a pintail across a frozen stream.* Photo © Jack Macfarlane

Facing page, top: *Black Lab puppies nursing.* Photo © William H. Mullins

Facing page, bottom: *Two young pups explore the smells of a pile of mallard decoys.* Photo © William H. Mullins

shallow sloughs and marshy potholes in the middle of the Mississippi, a half-mile west of the Batchtown Flats. Not once in the two-mile run to the island had there been any sign of ducks. The big island had seen a lot of red-letter days in the past, but this wasn't one of them. Not at first, anyway. "Which just goes to prove," Larry said, "that you never know about duck hunting."

He and Doc set their spread of 75 decoys and sat back with pipes and coffee, contemplating smartweed beds and quiet waters that remained steadfastly duckless.

Doc had his female black Lab, Windy, as usual. They came as a set. Larry had his black Lab, Bess—one of Windy's pups from six years earlier. Bess was swollen and miserable with a false pregnancy of the sort she often had after a heat period, but Doc assured Larry that the condition wasn't harmful, just uncomfortable. "I almost left Bess at home that day," Larry said, "but she sweet-talked me out of it. She wanted to go hunting so bad."

Full sunup, and still no sign of ducks anywhere in the sky. Then, Larry remembers, "The flats seemed to explode."

The eastern sky suddenly was skeined with ducks, newcomers that began working the decoy spreads in spite of the guns. Poultry all over the place—but not over Turner Island. There, peace and serenity reigned under a blue and empty sky.

Still, you hang around, never knowing when a few scraps might fall off the table. From out of nowhere, a lone mallard drake swung over the decoys in easy range. Larry took the shot, and Bess hit the water to fetch the day's first duck.

An hour later, two drake mallards and a hen came in off the river, answered the calls, and set their wings. Larry and Doc each dropped a greenhead, the birds were neatly retrieved, and tranquility again settled over their blind. Off to the east, it still sounded like a Juarez election. Through Doc's binoculars, flight after flight of ducks could be seen settling into the flats while our two heroes languished with cold guns and dry dogs. Slow torture of the worst kind, sitting under an empty sky while a hundred other guys were having powder fits less than a mile away.

It was more than any duck hunter could endure. Something had to be done even if it was wrong. In late morning Doc said, "Some of those guys are bound to have killed out by now. One of us should go back to the check station and see if we can get a blind over there in Hog Heaven . . ."

Doc won the toss, and Larry made the run to the landing alone. When he drove his pickup into the check station's parking lot, one look at the traffic told him the trip had been for nothing. As the flights of new ducks had come pouring in, the word had gone out and local hunters were waiting to take over hot blinds where limits had been filled. Larry joined the crowd, but at almost noon he was still twelfth on the list.

Enough of that. "Take my name off the list," he told the officer in

charge. "I'd rather be out there on Turner Island taking my chances than messing around here."

He took his time going back. Why hurry? There were ducks throughout the flats—but still none in sight around the island. He hid the boat and walked over to the blind where Doc was grinning the big hello.

"What are you so happy about?" Larry growled.

"Before I let you in," said Doc, "you have to guess what's in the blind that wasn't here when you left."

"Okay. So how many did you kill?"

"I got three blacks," Doc replied.

A Lab and its owner wait patiently in a duck blind. Photo © Lon E. Lauber

"What? I'm back there sweating out a line while you're sacking some black mallards?"

"Who said anything about ducks? Look at this."

On the floor of the blind lay Larry's Bess, with three black puppies no bigger than dressed teal. Soon after Larry had left, Bess had begun scratching under the seat of the blind—and once she began whelping, she made steady progress.

"She's had two of 'em within the last half hour," Doc explained proudly. "No problems, though. When you told me about her false pregnancy, I didn't pay much attention. This would have made the fourth time in the last two years, right?"

Right—except that Larry suddenly remembered the summer weekend when he'd attended a drawing for blind sites. Some of the hunters had brought their dogs and one big male Lab, in particular, had seemed smitten with Bess. A-huh . . .

"What are we going to do?" Larry asked.

"Just let nature take its course," Doc replied, "and keep hoping for ducks. No sense moving her and the pups as long as everything keeps going as it has so far."

At that point, a lone drake almost knocked their caps off. Doc dropped the greenhead just beyond the decoys, a cripple. "Grab your dog!" he said. "We don't want Bess to get wet!"

Larry seized a black neck with one hand and opened the door to the dog ramp with the other. Off and away went the Lab, with a surging splash.

"Reid!" yelled Doc. "You've got hold of Windy! That's Bess after that duck!"

No whistling or yelling could turn the gallant Bess. Lunging through the shallows, spraying mud and water widely, she finally caught the mallard when it became tangled in heavy smartweeds 75 yards from the blind. Bird in mouth, she trudged heavily back to a warm welcome.

It's doubtful that any swamp dogs, anywhere or anytime, ever had a more suitable welcome to the special world that would honor them and which, hopefully, they would honor in turn.

Doc was bent on keeping the pups as warm and dry as possible. A perfect solution was at hand. Three of the mallard drakes and an old towel were arranged on the roof of the blind to form a nest in the warm sun and dry willow branches. It's doubtful that any swamp dogs, anywhere or anytime, ever had a more suitable welcome to the special world that would honor them and which, hopefully, they would honor in turn.

"They nestled into those greenheads as if they were trying to retrieve them," Larry said. "And about then, pup number four arrived . . ."

So did more mallards—a christening gift from the Red Gods, some old hunters might say. As if drawn by the mewing puppies, ducks began coming out of the clear November sky in singles, pairs, small bunches. For the next hour or so, there was no thought of anything back in town, and the most important family problems were those being presented by Lady Bess. The dog chute had to be carefully guarded and blocked, for every time the hunters sounded their calls, Bess would be up and ready to go. As a fifth greenhead was added to

If there is a place in heaven for Labrador Retrievers (and I trust there is or I won't go) it'll have to have a brook right smack in the middle —a brook with little thin shoals for wading and splashing; a brook with deep, still pools where they can throw themselves headlong from the bank; a brook with lots of small sticks floating that can be retrieved back to shore where they belong; a brook with muskrats and muskrat holes; a brook with green herons and wood ducks; a brook that is never twice the same with surprises that run and swim and fly; a brook that is cold enough to make the man with the dog run like the devil away from his shaking; a brook with a fine spot to get muddy and a sunny spot or two to get dry.
—Gene Hill, *Tears and Laughter*, 1981

Left:*A yellow Lab emerges from the fog carrying a double retrieve.* Photo © Jack Macfarlane
Below: *Resting comfortably, two young Labrador pups are oblivious to the world.* Photo © William H. Mullins

The big-jowled black Lab "Cisco" pauses on the edge of a marsh. Photo © William H. Mullins

the bag, a fifth puppy was added to the little nest on the blind's roof. Soon there was a sixth puppy. The nest was being rapidly outgrown, but the wherewithal to enlarge it continued to drop out of the sky.

"This has to be some kind of record," Larry said as he moved puppies down into the blind to nurse.

"How so?" Doc asked.

"You ever heard of anyone hunting ducks with eight Labrador retrievers?"

The rest of the hunt was a happy confusion of filling limits and tending a half-dozen squirming objects that were as black and shiny as lumps of anthracite. With 10 drake mallards and six puppies, the hunters decided to call it a day, pick up, and report to the check station.

That establishment was basking in the sweet, smoky ambience that check stations always seem to have when the Brotherhood of the Drippy Nose has limited out. Grinning hunters with heavy strings of mallards and pintails stood about, still sharing the common adventure and the many marvels of the day. There was far more talking than listening.

With carefully calculated nonchalance, Larry laid out 10 mallards on the checking table.

"Looks like you guys did the right thing, going back to Turner," said the biologist in charge.

"You know it!" Doc broke in. "How about that? Ten greenheads and six blacks . . ."

Retrieving a black brant in Baja California, Mexico. Photo © Gary Kramer

"Six blacks? Are you crazy? That puts you guys way over the limit!"

"No limit on this kind of blacks," Doc grinned, and began hauling puppies out of the pockets of his big hunting coat. That shut off every other conversation in the room. It was the hit of the show, being played stage center to an audience of stern critics—all of whom gave rave reviews. Half the puppies were spoken for on the spot. After all, blood will tell—and how can any retriever whelped in a duck blind turn out to be anything but a top dog?

Out in the truck, Bess added pup number seven to the Lab population. An eighth and last puppy would arrive at home.

Larry settled back in his chair, I poured more coffee, and we both reflected in the warm afterglow of a well-told tale.

"A hunt to remember," I offered.

"Deed it was," said Larry. "Sure, Doc and I both remember when there were more ducks moving ahead of a northern front, or other hunts with odd twists of luck. Some mighty interesting dogwork, too."

"But I've never seen anything to match Bess' performance that day. It's been over 20 years but I still remember every detail. The way I figure it, the best duck hunts come in three parts: planning, doing, and remembering. I can't say which part is the best. Can you?"

No, I can't.

But if there's anything better than a perfect three-part hunt and eight new Labs, well, Larry and I will keep our mouths shut while you tell us about it.

Leaping into a Montana stream, this yellow Lab is off like a shot. Photo © Alan and Sandy Carey

Retriever trainers encourage owners to start their Labs early. Photo © Bill Buckley/The Green Agency

Above: *A typical day in the field with a Labrador retriever. The birds come into range, the hunter fires, and his Lab lunges for the retrieve.* Photo © Gary Kramer
Facing page: *After a difficult training retrieve, a Labrador waits patiently with the dummy he just bent over backwards to fetch.* Photo © William H. Mullins

Above: *A yellow Lab easily clears a bramble in a field.* Photo © Bill
Buckley/The Green Agency
Right: *A hunter and his yellow Lab exhibit the fruits of a successful hunt.*
Photo © Jack Macfarlane

I have never bought the Brooklyn Bridge or the Washington Monument, although I was once offered the latter at a bargain. Nor have I bought any hypothetical gold mines, ostrich farms, or the phony gilt-edged. I don't play poker, and I don't follow the ponies. If you should ask me to go to your bail, I would wag a moral forefinger and give you a whoso-goeth-surety-for-another look. And if you tried to high-pressure me, I would let fall an edifying precept or two and show you the exit. As you can see, I am a man of considerable moral fiber and high sales resistance. But, mister, have you got a dog to sell?
—Havilah Babcock, "I'm a Sucker That Way"

Old One-Ear

by Dion Henderson

Dion Henderson wrote from the heart of the Upper Midwest. He worked for the Associated Press's Wisconsin Bureau for more than forty years and held the position of bureau chief for fifteen years until his death in 1984. An author of eight books, including three novels, Henderson also wrote hundreds of articles for national magazines, including *Collier's*, *The Saturday Evening Post*, and *Field & Stream*.

This wonderful story, which appeared in the May 1953 edition of *Field & Stream*, tells the tale of a rather ugly Field Trial Champion, Old One-Ear, that comes through in the real world when a stellar performance matters most.

The sun sets over a black Lab, ankle-deep in frigid, late-autumn waters. Photo © William H. Mullins

EVERY MAN HAS to set up his own standards according to his lights, and his friends can either abide by them, or not. Peter knew exactly how mediocre his dogs were, and it made him react sharply to very good dogs. Maybe that was the trouble: his dogs never were quite as good as he wished they were.

The last dog Peter had was a good example. Sport was an atrocious workman, but Peter had had him seven years and was more stubborn about him at the end than he was at the beginning. That dog was a sort of miscellaneous retriever, and very casual at that. Late in the season, when the water was very cold, the dog would start a retrieve with a rush, get in about pastern-depth, then stop with a horrified expression and come back to the blind. Peter would not say anything, and of course neither would anyone else, but then another dog would be sent out. Peter would grin sardonically and say to his dog: "Look at that dang fool in there, courtin' rheumatiz and kidney trouble. You'll be running, Sport, when that dang-fool dog is too stiff to bend into bed."

When it was time for Sport, with unstiffened joints and well-preserved kidneys, to be pushed into the lap of his ancestors by the front end of a milk truck, we who hunted ducks with Peter conspired together. Presently Peter had a letter from an old friend, who ran quite a string of Labradors, saying he had a dog who was getting too hard to handle, a fighter but a passable workman when he felt like it and could Peter put him up.

Peter was against it. He said he didn't want any truck with a dog that came from any such hoity-toity background. I concurred with him, observing that a quarrelsome dog is a nuisance and, furthermore, if the no-account beast wasn't good enough for a competition string he wasn't good enough for fox meat. At that Young Peter bristled and said maybe that indicated the dog just had an uncommon amount of good sense, and he could very easily see how a dog might not get along very well with a bunch of dang fools. Immediately he sat down to write shipping directions.

He came all the way out of the box, a big dog, stretched some of the travel kinks out of his legs and looked us over with an expression made baleful by the scars and the missing ear.

We all went down to the railroad station with Peter the day the dog came in. He was in a regular travel box instead of a crate, and we could hear him growling as the baggage truck bumped and rumbled along the wooden platform to the depot. Peter opened the box and slipped a collar over the black head as it came out. It was easy to get the collar on because the dog had only one ear. The rest of his face was scarred up pretty well too. He came all the way out of the box, a big dog, stretched some of the travel kinks out of his legs and looked us over with an expression made baleful by the scars and the missing ear.

Peter almost beamed. "Ain't he the ugliest dog you ever saw?" he asked happily.

He had not yet stopped to think about the way the dog moved, the wonderful rolling driving gait of the high-bred Lab, and the way the dark eyes, not really baleful at all, watched your hands.

He had not yet stopped to think about the way the dog moved, the wonderful rolling driving gait of the high-bred Lab, and the way the dark eyes, not really baleful at all, watched your hands.

"I've seen prettier dogs," I admitted. Young Peter took it as a compliment.

"Old One-Ear," he said.

Then he turned to shut the door on the box and saw the name-plate. In front of the dog's name were the fateful letters: FTC.

"Field trial champion," Young Peter said in horror. "Field trial champion! By Godfrey, I've been swindled."

"A dog will instinctively try to sense your attitude, and respond accordingly. He'll learn your every gesture, your expression. It's said that if you're afraid, a dog can smell your fear."
Richard A. Wolters, Water Dog, *1964.* Photo © Jack Macfarlane

For a minute it seemed as though he might put the dog right back in the crate. But fortunately a depot cur dawdled by at the moment and the big Lab rumbled an instant, then went roaring to the end of his leash. Young Peter braced himself, looked again at the scars and the missing ear, and took Old One-Ear home.

"I'll give him a chance," he said, "to live down his past."

He said he would, but he didn't, not really. If One-Ear had a chance, he took it himself. Peter took him duck hunting, but didn't help him at all as far as handling went. The first time they went hunting One-Ear stayed in the boat all morning because Peter wouldn't tell him to go. Finally Peter's partner for the day became enraged and shouted "Fetch!" and One-Ear brought back seven ducks one right after the other. All Peter said was, "Dang show-off."

The first time I went out with them Peter allowed grudgingly that One-Ear marked his birds

A Lab poses by the license plate on its owner's truck. Photo © Jim Schlender

pretty well. He said this just after he had touched a high-flying redhead and the bird sailed stiffly downriver, across a sandbar and an island and another channel into the bulrushes. One-Ear brought it in, still alive, just five minutes after he left the boat.

"Yeah," I said, my voice an octave higher than usual with the strain of being non-committal, "fair-to-middling marker."

We had good shooting that day because there was big weather making. A gusting wind veered from north to northeast and back again, driving sheets of flat gray clouds ahead of it. You could feel winter in it, maybe snow up away from the river, and the chill that takes hold of you in the first few moments of morning, when you get out of the warm car and begin to load the boat, had not gotten completely out of my bones. Peter had a stall blind in one of the big sloughs, and most of the time I sat up forward on the shooting stage, where I could nurse the thermos and watch the birds working even when they weren't working for us.

One-Ear was getting used to the situation, learning what this strange new boss expected. He sat up in the boat watching the birds too, and when one was hit and there were no more birds in the sky he went out over the stern noiselessly as a mink, just sort of oozing up and out. Once when there was a bird down too far to one side where he couldn't see the fall, he turned, seventy yards away, looking back at

Peter. Peter looked at him and looked away.

Darn it, I thought. *What a waste of dog!* I gestured surreptitiously with one hand, and One-Ear took the signal immediately and a few minutes later made the find.

"I saw you," Peter said coldly. "I saw you do that. Dog with a college education. I'm too ignorant for a dog like that."

"No," I said. "Just too darned stubborn."

"Be that as it may," Peter said righteously, "you got to show me all that folderol makes sense."

So there it was, and what could I do? Sport wouldn't swim in cold water, but every day he'd go downtown and get the mail and bring it home—most of it, anyway. And the dog before that couldn't find a duck in his dog-house, but he'd caught a burglar in the hen-yard one time, and Peter never thereafter reproved him for losing a bird. Well, every man is entitled to his own opinion.

We were full on ducks by midafternoon, but Peter wanted to wait around for enough coot to make a pie. Most of them had moved out long since, but there was big water handy and some hung around all winter. Peter was still looking for the last coot when the wind changed again, and this time it meant business. We were a long pull from the car, but it was all downstream and not much cause for alarm at first. Somehow that wind was different, and the islands of vegetation in the slough were heaving as we worked out through them to the river.

We were just a little too late. Out there at the edge we could see the outer fringe of bogs breaking up, and already the main current beyond was black and furious and marked occasionally by debris. Peter heeled the motor open, and the boat charged out into the current, slanting downstream. You could feel the pounding through the boards. It was not like other times, even on the big river.

At first it looked as though we had plenty of lead on the current, but the current became faster and meaner; then when it was too late we could see we weren't going to get by.

There was an island in the channel that might have defied the river for a thousand years, or might have been made by the river in a year as a monument to a rowboat abandoned on a sand-bar, you never knew. Peter elected to cross the upper tip of the island instead of holding behind it, because the long curving point on the far shore where we had put the boat in was about even with the island, and going behind it meant we would have to fight current to land.

At first it looked as though we had plenty of lead on the current, but the current became faster and meaner; then when it was too late we could see we weren't going to get by. I was sitting there amidships like an idiot trying to light a cigarette in that wind, but not really thinking about cigarettes. When I saw we were not going to clear, I kept sitting there, because there was nothing to do. I still held the cigarette in one hand and the lighter in the other when the old tree stump reached up out of the dark water, and over we went.

I grabbed for something, the way a man will, and what I grabbed was my gun. This was pure instinct, which frequently plays a man false. Clinging to the gun, I pitched and wallowed in three feet of roaring water while the little tackle box that held food and fire and safety streaked away in the current. I saw it just as I pulled free of the water and dropped the gun, but the box was out of reach: a well-planned cork-lined box, guaranteed to bear a man's weight afloat, packed with canned heat, a knife, chlorine tablets, sandwiches and coffee.

Humping clumsily along the shore in waterlogged hip boots, I made one lunge for it, but the river spilled me and so I struggled up. Afterward I stood and watched the box whirl crazily out of sight somewhere down along the brushed-in point a quarter mile away, and I thought of all the hundred times I had packed and repacked that box and cursed its awkwardness in duffel and all the jeers and gibes I had suffered for its sake. I thought how all that had been for nothing, because now, the one time I needed it, it was lost.

The wind was howling down the valley of the big river, and the temperature was dropping toward the frost line. A decade ago a hundred men died of exposure in one night along this river.

I heard the dog barking, and started back toward the point of the island. Old One-Ear was partly in the water, barking at Peter, who still was in the water too, on his hands and knees except when the current knocked him down. I thought, *That is how a man can drown.* An instant later I saw that was what was happening. The dog was barking and trying to get hold of him, and Peter was trying to get up but couldn't.

When he was out of the water, he said, "It feels funny when you can't walk, especially when you have to."

"What happened? "

"I hit the tree," Peter said. "My leg is broken."

Maybe it was five minutes before we realized what that meant. The wind was howling down the valley of the big river, and the temperature was dropping toward the frost line. A decade ago a hundred men died of exposure in one night along this river.

It was late in the afternoon, late enough for everything to be turning gray except the gray-green streaks of wind in the far sky and the threat of snow. We were soaked to the skin and the last I saw of my lighter it was spinning in the air when the boat hit the tree. And Peter didn't smoke.

Facing page: *Inquisitive, confused, longing for attention, or just plain bored, this Lab looks over at his owner.* Photo © William H. Mullins

After helping him to a spot behind a dune where bushes helped screen the wind, I walked down the shore of the island again to where I could study the point. The box was there somewhere, a quarter mile away, and it might as well have been a hundred. I made a disgusted throwing-away gesture with my hands, and suddenly the dog was in front of me, watching my hands.

"No," I said. "You can't do anything." He waited, watching my hands as though he didn't believe me, and I said, "Can you?"

He didn't say anything, not aloud. He watched my hands.

"Maybe you can," I said to him. "If you remember how it was to be a really fine dog, and if you ever were as good as you remember, and if you want to be that good again and maybe twice as good, maybe you can."

He watched me. I tossed a soaked glove over in the brush, and he lunged for it and delivered very formally.

"All right," I said. "All right, then, Champion, that's what it smells like, and it's your show now. We'll start it off right. Finish!"

When I put my left hand on his neck, it was like pulling a trigger, and he went out across the first fifteen feet of water, leaving long, clawed pawprints in the sand.

He came around and sat down, hugging against my left leg. I left him there a moment, feeling the electric building up of tension, the gathering of power. When I knelt beside him, I could feel it in him, quivering, and when I gave him the line, the long, long line out into nowhere, it was all there at the firing-point. When I put my left hand on his neck, it was like pulling a trigger, and he went out across the first fifteen feet of water, leaving long, clawed pawprints in the sand.

Remembering how that current had clutched, I felt a numb surprise to see the dog swim it with powerful churning strokes, the mutilated black head swinging, watching. His power was much more apparent here where it was called for than it was in calm water. Once a branch slashed at him, and he veered with apparent ease but so violently that there was white foam around him.

It was all downstream. While I was wondering whether he could possibly make it he hit the point and went out on the land and turned to look back at me. It was a long, long way, just far enough to see the black dog against the sand. I stepped out knee-deep in current, braced myself so that he could see me outlined against the sky and signaled with one arm. He waited and I waved my arm again, and he swung off confidently that way. I did not know where the box was. I did not know whether he would pick it up if he found it. I was sure he could not carry it back against the current, anyway. But it was about all the chance there was.

The light was fading quickly now, but I saw the black dog back there on the sand, waiting. So it wasn't on that side, maybe. Try the other side. I signaled, but he couldn't see me any more. I swung my arm again and again, shouting futilely now. Then the wind opened a rift in the clouds behind me for an instant, and the dog saw, swung that way and disappeared in the treacherous tangle of river deadfalls along the current side of the point.

"What the heck are you doing?" Peter asked.

I shuddered, not from the cold because everything was too cold for that, but from the tight, hurt sound in his voice. "I put your dog ashore. Maybe someone will see him and start to wonder about us."

"Quit your kidding," Peter said. "It's getting dark, and there's no one for ten miles but a ranger in that fire tower and he can't see in the dark." He laughed a little. "Our chances depend on somebody seeing a black dog in the dark. Some chance."

I didn't answer him.

"Did you really think you could send him after a thing like that box?" Peter asked.

"You don't miss much," I told him. "It was worth a try. He's a field trial champion, Pete. That means a lot of handling to quite a few wins in a good many tough series. He's probably handled dummies all his life."

I walked back along the beach, but it was too dark now to see whether there was a dog on the far point. It didn't matter. I hoped he wouldn't get caught in the deadfalls and drown.

Walking back along the beach aimlessly, I wondered what you do with a man who has a broken leg and will freeze to death if he doesn't keep moving, but could not think of any answer. I walked on past Peter to the place we had foundered and halted suddenly, feeling that all-gone sickness in the belly when something impossible happens right in front of you.

One-Ear was coming toward me from the current, swimming high and furiously, the death struggle with the river making him blaze with rage instead of fright.

One-Ear was coming toward me from the current, swimming high and furiously, the death struggle with the river making him blaze with rage instead of fright. A length of debris hit him and rolled him in the dark water, and I saw the flash of white teeth in the black muzzle threatening the river, because a man or a dog must fight with the tools they have, and the heart and the rage and the teeth were what One-Ear had to fight with. Even then he was handicapped because he had the grip of the tackle box in his mouth.

When he came ashore, he came all at once, fighting free and

sprawling in the shallows. I jumped forward for the box, but he would not give it to me until he had gotten to his feet and sat down again to deliver it formally. I put my hand on him, but did not feel like saying anything.

"He found it down there and went all the way upstream along the shore because he knew he couldn't make it against the current." Peter said.

"I guess so, Peter."

After that it wasn't so bad. In a few minutes the canned heat had started some driftwood burning. I kept throwing wood on until the flames roared twenty feet high in the wind. In about a half hour, while we were drinking coffee and eating sandwiches, a launch came down from the dam to see whom the ranger had spotted trying to set fire to the river.

They took Peter aboard the launch and made him comfortable for the trip to the Coast Guard Station, and dropped me off at the point so that I could get the car. Just before I jumped ashore I said to Peter, "I'll take One-Ear along home with me."

"No," Peter said. "He'd better stay with me."

"You're going into the hospital boy."

"That's all right," Peter said indignantly. "Let's not overdo this thing. If that hospital's good enough for me to stay in, I guess even a field trial champion can stand it for a few days."

Looking a tad perplexed, a black Lab rests on the edge of an autumn cornfield.
Photo © William H. Mullins

A dog teaches a boy fidelity, perseverance, and to turn around three times before lying down.
Robert Benchley

Right: *With the tired eyes of a Bassett hound, this yellow Lab pup recuperates in a cozy spot.* Photo © Gary Kramer
Below: *Not only do rapidly growing Labrador pups need plenty of food, their water bowl is also king size, complete with a family of decoys.* Photo © Bill Buckley/The Green Agency
Overleaf: *From a timbered duck blind on the edge of a pond, a hunter and his Lab watch the sky for signs of their prey.* Photo © Lon E. Lauber

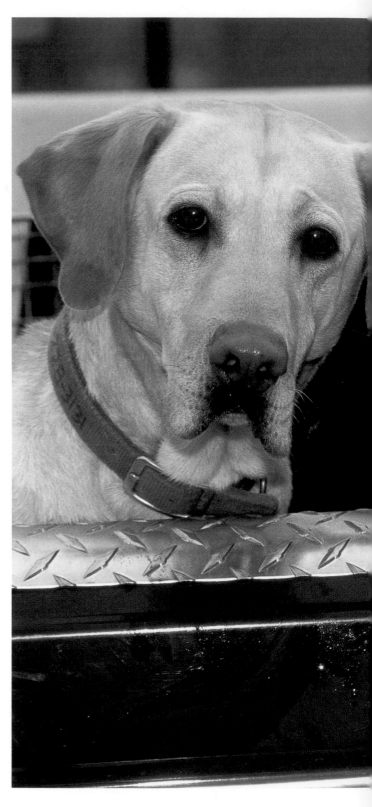

Above: *A yellow Lab puppy ready for action poses on a warm, summer day.* Photo © Alan and Sandy Carey
Right: *Offering a varied array of colors (and goofy looks), Lefty, Sage, and Nestle crowd the corner of a pickup bed.* Photo © William H. Mullins

Larry mixed another batch and suddenly [his Lab] Charlie rose up from under Larry's feet behind the bar and started to bark. Larry said, with a straight face, that Charlie was pretty good at mixing drinks and was reminding him that he had forgotten to add the Triple Sec to the Margaritas.
Gene Hill, *A Hunter's Fireside Book*, 1967

Above: *A chorus line of somewhat forlorn-looking Lab pups.* Photo © Alan and Sandy Carey
Facing page: *A chocolate Lab and his hunting companion in a duck blind.* Photo © Gary Kramer

I have sometimes thought of the final cause of dogs having such short lives, and I am quite satisfied it is in compassion to the human race; for if we suffer so much in losing a dog after an acquaintance of ten or twelve years, what would it be if they were to live double that time?
—Sir Walter Scott

of Miracles *and* Memories

by Bill Tarrant

Bill Tarrant is perhaps the strongest voice for the humane treatment of dogs in training—and everywhere else. An outspoken critic of training with intimidation, Tarrant bases his beliefs not only on morality but also on results. He unequivocally declares that "domination in gun dog training is dead" and adds that if a trainer bonds with his dog, "a look of disappointment on the trainer's face hurts an errant dog more than if he had been beat down with a 2 x 4."

For more than a quarter century, Tarrant has been the Gun Dog Editor for *Field & Stream*. In addition to hundreds of columns for the magazine, he is the author of eleven books, including *Bill Tarrant's Gun Dog Book: A Treasury of Happy Tails* and *Gun Dog Training: New Strategies from Today's Top Trainers*. The following piece originally appeared in the August 1983 issue of *Field & Stream*. For this piece, Bill Tarrant was awarded the Deepwoodsman of the Year award from the Outdoor Writers Association of America, an honor bestowed for the best outdoors story of the year. Tarrant wrote these words after a late-November day in the field with his Lab "Wasatch Renegade."

A Lab waits patiently by the edge of a pond on a frosty November morn. Photo © William H. Mullins

OLD GUN DOGS have stood the test of time and event and circumstance. They come now, slowly, and lay at foot or close to side, jowls flat, eyes faded with the fog of cataract, their muzzles and paws white or speckled salt and pepper. But they come. They want to be close.

They are great treasures, these old dogs. Lying there, they are more than themselves. They are us. Parts of us. A hill climbed together and the crimson leaves of sumac danced in the morning sunlight. The well looked in and the rock dropped; the chill of the dark hole seemed to go on forever before the splash was heard.

They are sweaty palms, for you were hosting your boss and he'd never gunned over a trained dog before. But Pup was so birdy you couldn't be sure he'd hold for shot and wing.

They are the iced mace of wind thrown by bad-dad winter, off to the north, blowing the red-leg mallards off their winter haunts. Blowing them south, flying like buckshot. And you're gripping Pup and whispering, "No head up," as you fit the duck call to your lips. It is so cold you know it will freeze to the skin. But you call. And the lead hen throws her body high, looking down and back, seeing the iced-in blocks pointing bill-up to the slate sky.

And now they come, shingles ripped loose from some old barn. The wind is driving them crazily toward your decoys, and you stand and the old gun barks and the dog launches. He's breaking ice and standing high in the water, though his feet don't touch bottom. And you wish you'd never shot. For nothing can live out there—not even Pup in the prime of his life. Yet he clomps the big bright drake and spins about, throwing water with his whipping tail. He comes for you—the drake covering his face—swimming by instinct, for he cannot see.

You're out of the blind now and running the bank, yelling out. The retriever comes to shore, not stopping to shake, and heads straight for you. But the black dog turns instantly silver. The water has frozen that fast. You take the duck and the dog shivers, his teeth chattering, and the pelvic-drive muscles convulse. Then he spins in the tall yellow grass: he runs and rubs the side of his jowls in the mud and stubble.

No duck is worth this—remember saying that?—and the two of you go back to the house. Back to the towel you rub over Pup and the fire you sit before as the wind makes a harmonica of your house-siding and whomps down the fireplace to billow the ashes.

But the duck does lay on the sideboard by the sink. You entered nature, went duck hunting, tricked the wildfowl to your trap, and the dog closed the door.

Still, you're sorry you went; but years later, when the smell of that day's wet fur is forgotten and the curled tail feathers from the mallard have long been blown from the fireplace mantle, you'll remember that retrieve and old Pup will come to side. You'll fondle his ears and the memory of that cold day and that single duck will become the most important thing that ever happened in your life.

For Pup is dying.

You can't see him, but you have to smile and call him to you. It may be the last time you ever touch his ear. But that's just part of it. You're dying, too (we all are, you know). Pup just will go first. As he always went first in the field and at the blind. You followed him, not the other way around. It was he who entered the unknown and learned its bareness or its bounty.

You love the old dog, for he lived your life. He was the calendar of your joy. Why, you could leap the stream when you got your first pup. Remember? And you could hunt all day. Cold? Bosh! And the apple in your pocket was all it took to fuel you from Perkin's fence to Hadley's barn—a limit of bobwhite later.

But now the arthritis hobbles you. And the cold. It seems to come and sit in your bones like an unwanted stranger.

So you don't just call Pup to side, you call your life. You run your fingers through your past when you fondle his ears.

So you don't just call Pup to side, you call your life.
You run your fingers through your past when you fondle
his ears.

You stand and go to the gun case. Why, the bluing's gone from that old Superposed. Then you remember when you bought it: long before Pup ever came into your life. And look at that duck call. There's no varnish left on the barrel. And the barrel is cracked! And the string that holds it. It was a country store back in the hills; you stopped for hamburger to feed Pup. And the duck call was in your pocket, just out of its cardboard box. You asked the proprietor for a piece of string and he went to the meat counter and drew off a yard of it. You were always going to get a bona fide, braided lanyard.

But that's like life. You were always going to. . . .

And there's Pup. He was not a going to. He was a was. Not a put-off till tomorrow. Pup was planned and bought and trained and taken to field. That happened. And the million dollars was never made, and you never became branch manager, and your kids didn't make it through college. But Pup did all you imagined for him.

Pup was your one success.

And he is dying.

How many pups ago was it your sweater fitted loose on your belly, and your belly was hard like the barrel of a cannon? But look at the sweater now. Stretched tight and tattered and faded. Why do you still wear it? There are Christmas sweaters still in their boxes on the shelf in the closet.

And the boots. Remember? They had to be just so. But look at them now. Toes out, scuffed, heels run over. And yet you shuffle about

Right: *The active life of a pup can be tiresome!* Photo © William H. Mullins

Below: *A soaking-wet Lab sporting a soiled bandana eagerly watches for its owner's signal.* Photo © Bill Buckley/The Green Agency

in them.

Is it because you're holding on to the past? Is it because looking back down the road means more than looking on up ahead? Is it because the birds you went with Pup to get were got? And now? What do they say? A bird in the hand is worth more than two—maybe that's it. Pup made you a bird-in-the-hand man.

Others, in those days, may have been two-bird hopefuls. But you and Pup did it. You went. No sunshine patriots then. No sir. That bird was in hand.

He's got bad teeth now, you know? Pup has. And let's admit it: his breath stinks. And look at him, great blotches of hair hang here and there like some derelict mountain sheep that's taken to roadside begging. And he does little but sleep—and pass gas. He does lots of that.

There are pups to be bought, you know? Why, ads are everywhere. And some say gun dogs have gotten better than ever. Or at least the training methods have gotten so sharp you can even bring a mediocre pup along.

It's always been you and Pup. And you'll wait till he's no more. But have you ever wondered? What will you be when he's gone?

But no. It's always been you and Pup. And you'll wait till he's no more. But have you ever wondered? What will you be when he's gone?

If he was the best part of your days, then what will there be when he's dead and buried? What will there be of you? Some grumpy old mumbler who sits by the fire and harrumphs at those who come to be kind?

No, not at all. For you were a gun dog man and you went to field. Your Pup was the best gun dog you ever saw. And you watched the flash of the great black dog as he leaped through bramble and you saw him once atop the hill. How far away was he on that cast? A half mile! And all you must do is close your eyes; better yet, just go to the window and watch the falling leaves. Pup's out there. He's by the gate. See him? And he's leaping that way he always did, urging you to get on with it. And he darts now, to the field, and sniffs the passing mice, the dickey birds.

And then you're with him, the weight of the gun reassuring in your grasp. Your stride is strong and the wind bites your cheek, but you laugh and blow the white steam of cold. Always you can do this, just standing at the window—for you did this.

What of the smell of straw at the old duck blind and pouring the coffee from the Thermos. Then learning how to pour the coffee from the steel cup so you could put the cup to your lips. And you never knew why the pouring made the cup manageable.

And the pride in your homemade decoys, watching them run to the end of their cords and spin about, ducking their heads and bobbing toe drip water from their bills.

And off to the left, in that stand of multiflora rose: Hear him! The cock pheasant *car-runks*. Bright as brass he is. And you could heel Pup out of the duck blind and go get him, but you like his sass. You like his arrogance. And the fact that anything that gaudy can live out there in the back of your place.

And what of the morning you and Pup were sitting there? Duck hunting for you didn't mean shooting ducks. It meant being there. Hearing the russle of your heavy canvas pants and the tinkle of the dog whistles and calls as they danced on your chest. Blowing in cupped hands, beating them against the sides of your chest. And standing and stomping on the wood pallets you brought in because the water rose with the late rains. And for that moment you and Pup were silent and the redtailed hawk landed, right above both of you, on a naked limb.

You were ornery. Jumped up, you did, and yelled, "Hey, Hawk!" And the hawk was so discombobulated he hurled himself to the air with a great squawk, leaving a white stream all over your blind as he beat his departure. But it was still funny, and you sat in the draping of hawk feces—and laughed.

That's what a gun dog comes to be for us. An enricher of life. Something to take ordinary moments and make them miraculous.

Not another single living thing had that moment but you and Pup and the hawk. And the three of you made that moment momentous forever. The hawk is gone and Pup is going but that moment makes you all vibrant and alive. And in a way it makes you important. Who else ever had an exclusive moment?

And if Pup had not taken you to field, you'd not have had it. So he lays there now, that generator of meaning and memory. That's what a gun dog comes to be for us. An enricher of life. Something to take ordinary moments and make them miraculous.

That's why the love for Pup is so great. What matter if he passes gas and has bad breath and moans in his sleep. He's earned his transgressions. And he tells us of our own end. For sharing the best with him, we must now share the worst with him, and we lie there, too.

But dog men push that away. Their Pup was a springer spaniel, you know. Oh, how happy he was afield. Why the stub of his tail couldn't be tallied as it wagged. And it wagged that way when idle or working. He was just that happy. And he made the man happy. For happiness is infectious, and there's no known cure. Not even disaster. For you'll walk around the knowledge of disaster to peek in memory at that happy tail.

And that man's Pup was a beagle. A mellow-voiced ground snorter if ever there was one. The bow legs, all that massed muscle. And how he used to launch the rabbit and then dart out in pursuit, giving the man instructions—Loud Instructions!—on when to shoot.

But that's not the Pup I was thinking of. No. That Pup was your cocker with thick hair the color of wheat tassels; he'd rut to launch the bird, down in the mud, going under the high-water log. And up he'd come with that smashed face, little mud balls hanging from his silver whiskers, and in a turn—which was more like a complete flip—he'd

tell you with his body signal there was nothing down there and you'd best be off.

But who am I to talk like this? You know your Pup better than I ever could. For there was just the two of you—oh, maybe a hawk! And what happened can never happen again. No man and dog could ever be that rich, that lucky, that blessed again.

Yet, each year several million new pups are taken into American homes, into American hearts. All on the knowledge that there are some miracles and memories left out there yet.

Above: *An insulated pair hunts waterfowl along a Montana river.* Photo © Alan and Sandy Carey Overleaf: *"A stylish dog is the Labrador, a handsome dog, a top-notch worker, and a loyal friend."* *Rowland Johns,* Our Friend the Labrador, *1934.* Photo © Bill Buckley/The Green Agency

Above: A Lab waits ankle-deep in choice Idaho muck. Photo © William H. Mullins

Right: *Labs have an acute sense of smell. The British employed Labradors to sniff out land mines during the Second World War.* Photo © Lon E. Lauber

Above: *Two hunters and their tail-wagging Lab hunt sharptail grouse on the North American Great Plains.* Photo ©
Gary Kramer
Facing page: *Though not as popular for field work as black Labs, yellow Labs are talented waterfowl retrievers.* Photo ©
Bill Buckley/The Green Agency

Most behavioral scientists agree that the fairly recent development of the Frisbee brought out the full potential of the Labrador.
Gene Hill

Below: *In pursuit of an elusive tail, this Labrador pup assumes a position that would make a master contortionist envious.* Photo © William H. Mullins
Right: *Two Idaho Labs hang over the edge of a pickup bed.* Photo © William H. Mullins

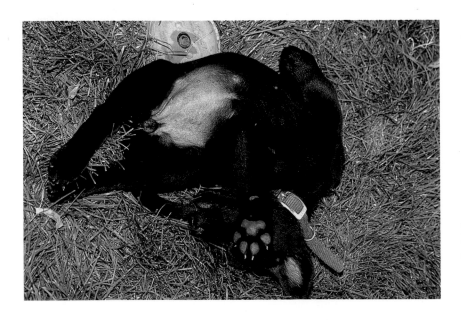

After a long day in the field, a sleepy black Lab rests on its owner's arm. Photo © Lon E. Lauber